BOOKS N BROS

BOOKS N BROS

44 INSPIRING BOOKS FOR BLACK BOYS

SIDNEY KEYS III

GET CREATIVE 6

GET CREATIVE 6
An imprint of
Mixed Media Resources
19 W. 21st Street, Suite 601
New York, NY 10010

Editors
TODD HUNTER
PAMELA WISSMAN

Art Director
IRENE LEDWITH

Designer
DANITA ALBERT

Cover Illustration by
MARLA BONNER

Interior illustrations by
ESTHER STIMPHAT @KJA artists
and MARLA BONNER

Photos pages 8-9
MENA DARRE PHOTOGRAPHY

Chief Executive Officer
CAROLINE KILMER

President
ART JOINNIDES

Chairman
JAY STEIN

Library of Congress Cataloging-
in-Publication Data available upon
request.

1 3 5 7 9 10 8 6 4 2

First Edition

Printed in China

"For every door that's been opened to me, I've tried to open my door to others. And here is what I have to say, finally: Let's invite one another in. Maybe then we can begin to fear less, to make fewer wrong assumptions, to let go of the biases and stereotypes that unnecessarily divide us. Maybe we can better embrace the ways we are the same. It's not about being perfect. It's not about where you get yourself in the end. There's power in allowing yourself to be known and heard, in owning your unique story, in using your authentic voice. And there's grace in being willing to know and hear others. This, for me, is how we become."

—Michelle Obama, Becoming

DEDICATION

To our family, our growing community of Bros and their families: Thank you for supporting us as a son-mother duo. It is with you that we have been able to disrupt stereotypes and build legacies based on family, society, entrepreneurship, and imagination—permitting what is possible, allowing ourselves to become who we are called to be.

TABLE OF CONTENTS

INTRODUCTION

Growing up, I never imagined books would become such a big part of my life. I mean, hey, it's gotten to be so that I'm now writing a book about books. A quote by Rudine Sims Bishop perfectly sums how I feel about books. She refers to them as windows and mirrors:

"Books are sometimes windows, offering views of worlds that may be real or imagined, familiar or strange. These windows are also sliding glass doors, and readers have only to walk through in imagination to become part of whatever world has been created or recreated by the author. When lighting conditions are just right, however, a window can also be a mirror. Literature transforms human experience and reflects it back to us, and in that reflection we can see our own lives and experiences as part of a larger human experience. Reading, then, becomes a means of self-affirmation, and readers often seek their mirrors in books."

Books have been modes of transportation for my life over the last six years and more! How? Well, honestly, this is where it all began.

In the summer of 2016, I was returning home to St. Louis, Missouri from Apple Valley, California where I spent a few weeks with my grandparents. I was just ten years old and this was my first time traveling alone without my mom and on an airplane at that! But traveling

alone wasn't as scary as I thought. Flight attendants accompanied me throughout the airport and on the plane. I met another UM, (unaccompanied minor) and he was super cool. We played games and just made the best of the flight! I had no idea that a major life changing surprise would be waiting for me back in St. Louis.

As my mom excitedly picked me up from the airport, she mentioned how much she missed me and that she had so many fun things in store. A few days later, I was presented with the surprise. I thought we were going to an arcade, one of my favorite restaurants, or the mall, but we arrived at a small, local, Black-owned bookstore; the only African American children's bookstore in St. Louis to be exact! This bookstore is called EyeSeeMe, and the name says it all. As I almost disregarded my mom's efforts, I shortly became captivated by everything I saw once we entered EyeSeeMe.

We pulled the door open together, the bell attached to the door announced our entrance and the owner greeted us with a smile. As my mom spoke to the owner, I was captivated by all the black and brown faces I saw on the book covers, on wall posters; from comic book characters, historical figures, spiritual figures, and more! And they all looked like me.

Normally, going into a bookstore isn't the most exciting thing to do, especially for a ten-year-old. But this moment was special because I was never really exposed to African American literature

Top photo from left to right: Dredyn Lilly, Ryan "Woo" Jackson Jr., and Camryn Pickens.
Bottom photo: I'm reading to book club members in St. Louis at a meetup hosted by EyeSeeMe Bookstore.

at school. I would get to see a few books around Black History Month. But even then, the books were about Dr. Martin Luther King Jr. or Rosa Parks or some other well-known historical figure. Don't get me wrong, they are all amazing people who we should know. It's just that we were reading these stories every year as if there were only a handful of contributors to the Black experience.

As a kid, you want to see more books that relate to you, books about kids that look like you, and not just Jimmy and his dog and stories like that. The first book that I actually read in that bookstore was *Danny Dollar Millionaire Extraordinaire*, by Ty Allan Jackson, a book about a kid who creates a successful business. I picked up the book because the kid on the cover looked like me. Then I started reading it and I just couldn't put it down.

Something extremely revolutionary was happening. My mom noticed my excitement and she was excited as well! She was so excited that she asked the owner, "Is it okay if I go LIVE on social media to capture your store and show support?" At the time, my mom was blogging nationally and was pretty good at it. She'd always support entrepreneurs from all over the country, but even this day surprised us all. My mom went live on social media, capturing me reading, showing off the store, and guess what? That video went viral with over 65,000 views! My mom asked me, "What do you want to do with this moment? You can either have

In 2017, I was invited to be a guest on Steve Harvey's daytime talk show in Los Angeles by Mrs. Marjorie Harvey to discuss my efforts to amplify African American literature. Oprah Winfrey also virtually chimed in to offer some special words of encouragement.

I was invited to speak at WE Day Community: St. Louis in 2019 and met fellow speaker Martin Luther King III.

January 2020, Mom and I were guests on Good Morning America in honor of Martin Luther King Jr. Day. Robin Roberts surprised us with a $10,000 donation from Wells Fargo to help fund Books N Bros.

your fifteen minutes of fame on social media or truly make an impact." I asked the bookstore owners if they knew of a book club that I could join that focused on African American literature. The only one they could offer was called Nerdy Girls. Let's just say I wasn't the best fit to join that club. So I chose to make an impact. I responded to mom, "I want to start a book club . . . for boys like me who want to learn more about African American literature!"

"What would you name this book club?" my mom asked. I responded with a smile, "I'll name it Books N Bros!"

In that moment, books transformed the trajectory of my life, from flying to cities I never imagined, from New York, to Los Angeles, to the

Washington, D. C. area, all to talk about books and inspire others to see the importance of literacy.

Think there's no way books can change your life? Think again. No matter your age, zip code, or gender, you can do what your heart desires. But I know what you're thinking, "Where do I start?" Think back to how my mom presented the possibility to me. Here are three tips:

• Identify the problem. My mom always says if there's a void that needs to be filled, you fill it!

• Identify the solution that makes sense to YOU. We're all different for a reason. I created what makes sense for ME. You can definitely create a positive project to impact others looking for a solution from YOU.

• Realize that you don't need to do it alone.

You need a grownup to help with paperwork and to give you great advice along the way because building new possibilities is hard work!

A LIFT FOR LITERACY

I started Books N Bros in the summer of 2016. Our first meetup was at the EyeSeeMe bookstore outside of St. Louis. They allowed us to host meetings in a back room and we were able to sell snacks.

Soon word about the book club began to travel locally and we started to grow. The bookstore would eventually become too small for our meetups. So then we reached out to a Microsoft center inside of a mall and they agreed to let us have our meetings there. Those days were fun times because we would pull out Xboxes after each meetup and play video games. Books always came first, though. The Microsoft center is where Books N Bros really became a type of brotherhood. It was a place where we could bond.

Just before the book club took off in a big way, I had a moment of doubt. It was Superbowl Sunday and we were still meeting at the Mircrosoft center. Before

After a successful book club meetup, members of Books N Bros in St. Louis, pose together with their limited edition copies of Sidney's MARVEL Hero comic, The Spectacular Sidney.

the meeting, I had a feeling that I should cancel and reschedule it. But then I told myself, "no, football players need to read too. I'm going to stick to the date." My worst fear came true. We only had maybe three boys show up. At this time, we were averaging between 10 and 15 Bros at each meetup. This was truly a blow.

After the meeting, as we were packing our books and snacks, I told my mom that "I don't wanna do this anymore. Nobody's supporting." But my mom was having none of it. She told me, "Sidney, let's just give you one more month because I don't quit things easily. And I don't want you to. If it's the same result next month, then we can move on."

Literally, days later, my mom gets a notification on Instagram that I was highlighted in the Huffington Post. She couldn't believe it and neither could I. The next month we packed out the Microsoft store. There were kids from the front to the back wanting to learn about Books N Bros. We even had someone from the local NBC news channel who came out to do a story on the book club.

The Huffington Post feature was the start of something big. Other media like *Ebony* magazine reached out, and celebrities were posting about me on their social media pages. Almost overnight we grew from a book club that only a few people knew about to becoming a viral sensation nationwide.

We eventually outgrew the Microsoft center and moved our meetups to the Ferguson Youth Initiative in Ferguson, Missouri. The youth initiative is all about creating an empowering environment for youth and Books N Bros was a perfect fit. It was just the kind of fun and uplifting program for young African American boys that the city needed, especially after what happened to Michael Brown in 2014 and because tensions around young Black boys still lingered. We were tapping into something real.

We also decided to incorporate a component to the book club called "Big Bros." They were men who would help facilitate our meetups and lead important conversations. It was great to have the Big Bros around because they were role models for us young Bros.

Time has gone by so fast since that first visit to EyeSeeMe bookstore. It feels like a blur. As I write this book, Books N Bros is now mostly virtual. We moved online to offer a way to host more people from all across the country, and even the world. Since 2016, Books N Bros has reached over 700 boys nationally and internationally. The book club really has grown beyond my wildest dreams.

What I haven't shared so far is that in elementary school I would get teased for having a really bad stutter. Reading was a way for me to escape and I was able to visualize things and play out all the events clearly. I guess that's when my love of reading started. But my love of books started that day at EyeSeeMe when I saw all of those books with people on them who looked like me.

I assembled this reading guide because I wanted to share my love with you. I hope these books will transform your world the way they did mine. The books featured were the foundation of the Books N Bros book club. They are organized by category: History; Biographies; Novels, Short Stories, and Poems; and Comics, Graphic Novels, Superheroes, and Science Fiction. The best part is that there are so many more books that we have yet to read…and I can't wait.

This reading guide is more than a book about books. It's a book about you. Enjoy.

CHAPTER 1 : HISTORY

People ask me, "What's your favorite school subject?" You'd probably assume my answer will be ELA (English Language Arts), English, etc. But history is my favorite subject. I love to learn about the origins of things. It helps me understand different cultures better. And the traveling I've been able to experience has also opened my eyes to the importance of knowing the history behind people, places, and things.

For example, one of my favorite authors is a native of my hometown, St. Louis. She unfortunately passed away in 2017, but before she did, I was fortunate to learn of her writings and teachings, and introduce many of her books to my Books N Bros book club! Her name is Patricia C. McKissack and she's a literary treasure.

I learned about McKissack from my mother, and she learned of her from her mother, my grandma, who has had an impact on my appreciation of books and history. My mom told me that she met McKissack at the Missouri History Museum when she was a kid! That's how history is shared and stories are told, right? From our own experiences and from those closest to us. The books I'm sharing here are books about history that I never knew I needed but when I read them, I was excited to share them with my Bros and now with you too!

OTHER BOOKS FOR BROS BY
KADIR NELSON

If You Plant a Seed

He's Got the Whole
World in His Hands

Nelson Mandela

HEART AND SOUL

The History of America and African Americans

Written and Illustrated by **KADIR NELSON**

Think about the things we learn in American history class. We learn about the Declaration of Independence, slavery, war, voting rights, and more. Well, in *Heart and Soul*, author and artist, Kadir Nelson, gives us another perspective of the United States, from colonial days through the civil rights movement, as well as facts about Black innovation, revolution, reconstruction, abolition, and more, highlighting the good with the bad.

The story is told through the eyes of a 100-year-old African American female narrator whose ancestors came to the U.S. on slave ships and who lived to cast her vote for Barack Obama, the first African American president. The colorful images make it worth every page flip, and it is a great book for readers of different ages and backgrounds.

Storytellers like Nelson are appreciated because even though these topics may be taught in school, it doesn't mean history has fully been told or includes diverse perspectives. So how do we verify if history is being told accurately? Nelson helps us answer that question. You can visit the back of this book to see a two-page timeline of all the events referenced, a full-page bibliography, and a four-page index. In later editions, he provides discussion questions for the classroom and interview questions he answers as well.

This a very well-thought-out book! But when you're an award-winning illustrator, Coretta Scott King Book Award author and illustrator recipient, and your art has been viewed in galleries and museums around the world, it's expected you'll have things in order.

Heart and Soul shows that in our struggles for freedom and equal rights, African Americans have helped, and continue to help, our country achieve its promise of liberty and justice for all.

WHAT COLOR IS MY WORLD?

The Lost History of African American Inventors

Written by **KAREEM ABDUL-JABBAR** and **RAYMOND OBSTFELD**
Illustrated by **BEN BOOS** and **A. G. FORD**

This *New York Times* bestseller contains the lost history of little-known African American inventors thanks to basketball legend Kareem Abdul-Jabbar and Raymond Obstfeld. It highlights the contributions of African Americans to science, medicine, and technology with the story of thirteen-year-old twins, Herbie and Ella, who take us through their journey of learning about amazing inventors that we may have never heard of! That is exactly what drew me to grab this book in the first place.

The first invention that got my attention was the light bulb. In school we're taught that Thomas Edison invented the first light bulb. But according to this book, "Historians list twenty-two inventors of incandescent lamps before Thomas Edison." It is said that Edison used his business savvy, popularity, and skill set as an inventor to become successful as the face behind the invention of the light bulb. But some of the unsung African American heroes behind the success of electricity and other inventions are Dr. Henry T. Sampson, Lewis Howard Latimer, and Granville T. Woods (called the "Black Edison").

Let's highlight Dr. Henry T. Sampson. In 1967, Dr. Sampson was the first African American to earn a PhD in nuclear engineering. Then in 1971, he was recognized for inventing the gamma electric cell, which basically transforms electricity from radiation. How cool!

Later, we learn of Lewis Howard Latimer. Among his many achievements, Thomas Edison hired Lewis Latimer to work for him and Latimer helped him with the patenting application process, protecting Edison's patents, as well as creating a huge library on all information about incandescent lighting.

Then there's Granville T. Woods, the inventor of the steam-boiler furnace for trains, but he's most famous for inventing the induction telegraph. What's that? The induction telegraph allowed trains to send and receive messages from railroad stations while traveling! Much differently from Latimer,

Woods was asked to work for Thomas Edison but refused and continued working for himself. These are just a few of the inventors highlighted in this book!

SCRAPS OF TIME

Written by **PATRICIA C. MCKISSACK**
Illustrated by **GORDON C. JAMES**

Imagine learning about Black history from kids of the 1920s and beyond. For example, what if you could learn about the Harlem Renaissance or Negro League baseball from the kids who were able to experience these historical moments in real life? Well, this concept of Black history storytelling is expressed in Patricia C. McKissack's Scraps of Time series which is one of my favorites. McKissack was born in Tennessee but lived most of her life in my hometown, St. Louis!

I learned about Patricia C. McKissack from my mother, my grandmother, and my first visit to EyeSeeMe bookstore in St. Louis. I wanted to meet McKissack but unfortunately she passed away less than a year after I learned of her legacy. In her honor, and due to popular demand from my book club members (my Bros), we read the entire Scraps of Time book series. Specifically, *Scraps of Time 1937: The Home-Run King*, is my favorite of the series. The book is written from the perspective of kids attending a Negro League baseball game full of superstars, but plot twist, they have to sneak into the game because they're kids right? This is an eye-opening story for those who may not know that baseball games were once for white-only teams.

Then, there's *Scraps of Time 1928: A Song for Harlem*. What do you think this book is about? You guessed it! The Harlem Renaissance, but from a kid's point of view. Lilly Belle, a twelve-year-old from Smyrna, Tennessee, tells her story through the writings of journals she left behind for her niece to share with generations to come. Lilly Belle expresses throughout the book the culture change she experienced moving from a small town like Smyrna to Harlem, a neighborhood in New York City. She learns from some of the greats in creativity, literacy, arts, and entrepreneurship. From A'Lelia Walker (a

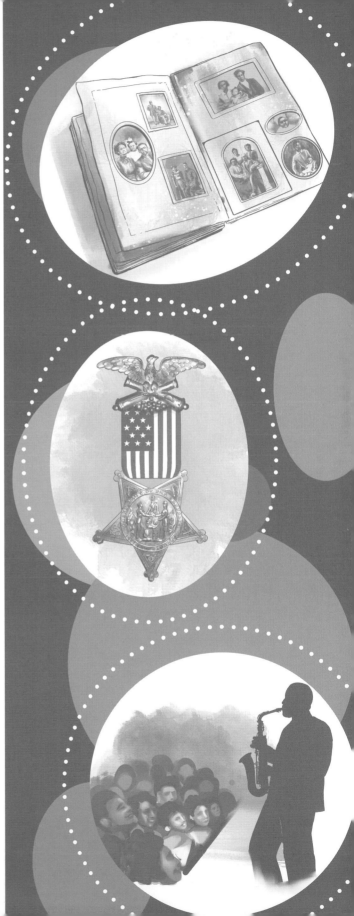

(a businesswoman and the daughter of the legendary Madame C. J. Walker) to the literary treasure, Zora Neale Hurston—because Lilly Belle attended a writer's workshop taught by Hurston and hosted by Walker. As I'm growing up a kid entrepreneur, and I know so many creative people and business owners, this specific *Scraps of Time* is one of my favorites as well.

OTHER BOOKS FOR BROS BY PATRICIA C. MCKISSACK

A Long Hard Journey
The Story of the Pullman Porter

Madam C.J. Walker

The Dark-Thirty
Southern Tales of the Supernatural

Langston Hughes
Great American Poet

WE ARE THE SHIP

The Story of Negro League Baseball

Written and Illustrated by **KADIR NELSON**

This book, *We Are the Ship,* tells stories of Negro League baseball in the United States from the 1920s in a way that makes you feel like you're in the stands. Kadir Nelson's artwork really shows Black baseball athletes in a positive light. It

pulls at your heart as he's able to truly capture the emotions that the players may have felt at that time. I have always loved to read but I never appreciated the illustrations until I experienced this artist's work.

In a time where we appreciate highlighting unsung heroes, I appreciate that Kadir names so many Black baseball players from that time. You have players like Charlie Grant, Pete Hill, Rube Foster, Hank Aaron, Tony Gwynn, and more!

In a very heartfelt author's note, Kadir even mentions, "I hope that I have done justice to these somewhat forgotten men and given them the tribute that they deserve. I have tried to honor them, to portray them as the heroes they were, and to further solidify their place in history. I hope that the reader will agree."

As a reader, I wholeheartedly agree that Kadir Nelson has done an awesome job with showing us the superpowers of Negro League baseball. After reading *We Are the Ship,* I wish I was alive to experience the beauty of what it was like to see so many men who look like me excelling in baseball.

Growing up in St. Louis, my mom would take me to Cardinals games every once in a blue moon. Baseball is a pretty big deal in St. Louis. Sometimes it'll seem like the entire city is at the game! In my experience, most of the players and fans didn't look like me. So imagining what Negro League baseball was like, as a young Black boy who enjoys baseball, I appreciate Kadir for illustrating what seems like a fantasy world.

KIDS READ WHAT THEY LIKE

If you know a child or student is interested in sports, try getting him or her a book about sports. For example, you could gift them with a copy of *We Are the Ship*, which offers an awesome story about baseball with vibrant illustrations to match. This would also be a great book for a kid who's into art! Kadir Nelson is an artist who has other artwork that many have seen around the world and if I were an artist, I'd be inspired to create illustrations for books as well!

OTHER BOOKS FOR BROS BY
KADIR NELSON

Change Has Come
An Artist Celebrates Our American Spirit

Baby Bear

The Village That Vanished

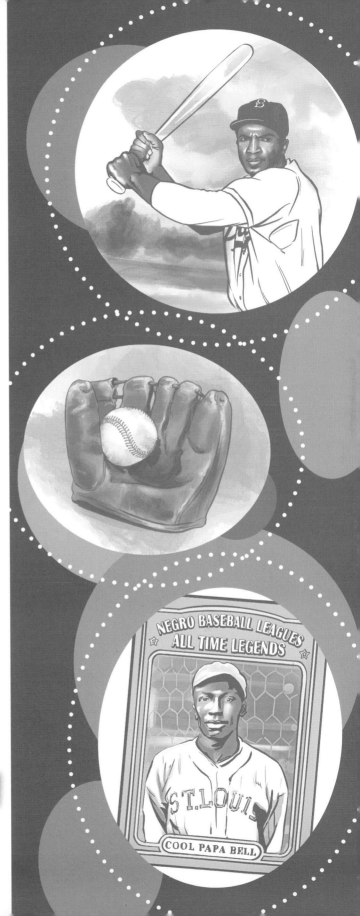

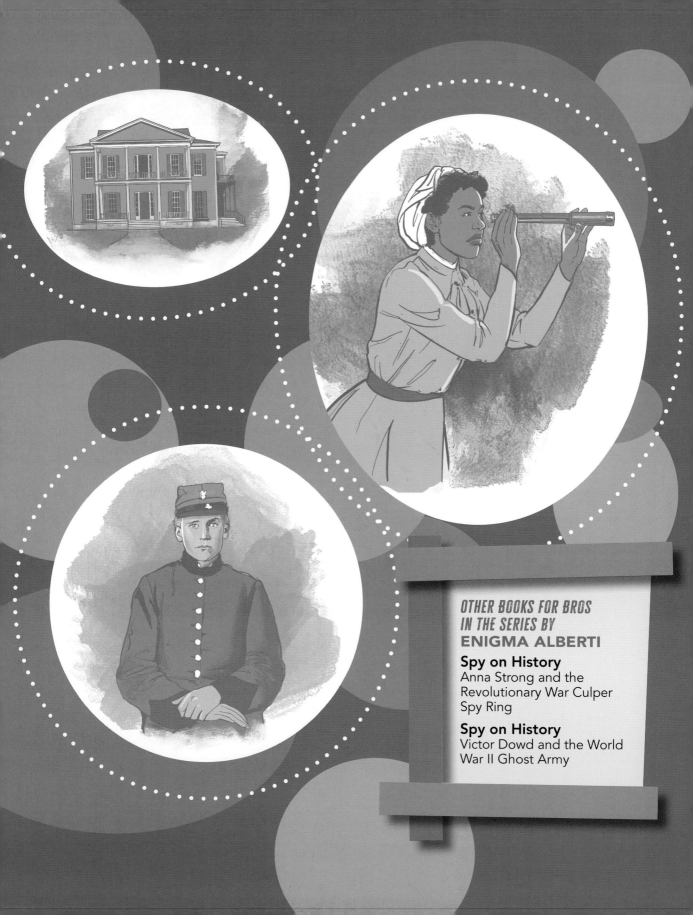

SPY ON HISTORY

Mary Bowser and the Civil War Spy Ring

Written by **ENIGMA ALBERTI**
Illustrated by **TONY CLIFF**

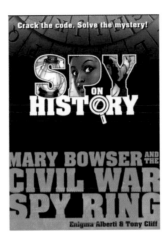

As a kid, I've always been fascinated with both history and adventure. Exploring this mysterious true story of a Civil War spy ring through the secret diary of Mary Bowser, an African American spy for the Union who worked as a maid in the mansion of Confederate Jefferson Davis, was a different type of adventure I never knew I needed.

Every time I'd watch spy cartoons or movies, the characters were never people of color. And most of the time, the spy was a man. Mary Bowser really changed the face of what a spy looked like to me! Bowser was a female, African American spy!

What makes this even cooler? The layout of the book takes you on a step-by-step journey in literary form. When I first opened this book, I recognized that there are tools needed to crack this mystery. As you open the first pages, you'll find an envelope sealed to the book with a note, and other tangible tools to decode this mystery. And there's another envelope in the back!

As a kid who loves adventure and history, this book had me in a place of excitement as soon as I opened it for the first time. This book was also a hit with my Bros because of the way you can interact instead of only reading. My Bros enjoyed reading it together in small groups, while adding a competitive edge to see who could crack the mystery first. The more that I think about it, the interactive format of this book encourages kids who normally don't read to actually enjoy reading!

It makes me think. I always get asked the question, "So how would you inspire teachers and parents who are trying to help increase interest in reading?" I always say that you should know who you're trying to reach first. Don't force what you like to read on your kids or students. Just because you like it doesn't mean it will capture the attention of younger readers. Most of the time, we like to read, we just don't want to read what we're not interested in.

OTHER BOOKS FOR BROS BY
CAROLE BOSTON WEATHERFORD

Moses
When Harriet Tubman Led Her People to Freedom

Freedom on the Menu
The Greensboro Sit-Ins

Freedom in Congo Square
Voice of Freedom
Fannie Lou Hamer: The Spirit of the Civil Rights Movement

The Roots of Rap
16 Bars on the 4 Pillars of Hip-Hop

UNSPEAKABLE
The Tulsa Race Massacre

Written by **CAROLE BOSTON WEATHERFORD**   Illustrated by **FLOYD COOPER**

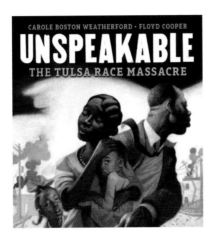

Imagine a children's book with amazing illustrations that tells the explicit truth about what happened in Tulsa, Oklahoma in 1921—one of the worst incidents of racial violence in American history when a white mob attacked the Black community of Tulsa's Greenwood district. It showcases legendary efforts made by hardworking Black men and women before the tragic event of 1921. We get a chance to envision what Dreamland Theatre that served African American audiences looked like, escape into the wealth of the Greenwood area, and get a beautiful glance at Black Wall Street and all it had to offer.

This is a book for the entire family to explore. Talking about something so terrifying is not easy for anyone. I believe that this book properly states the facts, while sharing the city's history in a beautiful way.

Technically, the book is for readers ages 8–12. As someone who is in high school, however, I think this book appeals to readers of all ages. *Unspeakable: The Tulsa Race Massacre* definitely speaks to those who are ready to unveil the truth of racial history in the United States. What I really enjoyed about the book is learning about the lives of African Americans who were successful and did all they could to make a way for themselves during difficult times.

So many people believe false narratives of Black and Brown people in America that implies we can only be athletes, entertainers, or in poverty, when in fact, that is not what we're limited to at all. This book is important because it provides a narrative about Black and Brown people that is positive, uplifting, and deserves more attention.

If you're a parent (or someone who deals with kids) and want an easy outlet to explain the unspeakable event to your child (or niece, nephew, student, grandchild, etc.), this is the book for you. *Unspeakable: The Tulsa Race Massacre* not only introduces young readers to this tragedy, but it concludes with a call for a better future. As a teenager, I even learned more than I expected. It's a great read for everyone!

THE PORT CHICAGO 50

Disaster, Mutiny, and the Fight for Civil Rights

Written by **STEVE SHEINKIN**

The Port Chicago 50 is an amazing read that tells the little-known story of fifty Black sailors accused of mutiny by the U.S. Navy during World War II. Many Black sailors were transported to a United States naval base in San Francisco called Port Chicago where they transported and loaded bombs and ammunition into ships bound for American troops in the Pacific. However, they were never taught how to safely do so. On July 17, 1944, there was an explosion in the port killing 320 servicemen and injuring many more. Surviving servicemen were taken to another nearby base and ordered to proceed back to work. They refused and protested the terrible working conditions they were given, but the officers accused them of mutiny and threatened to sentence all those who did not comply to a firing squad which intimidated a lot of them to retreat. Many of the sailors were intimidated, except for fifty servicemen, including Joseph Small, a young Black man who demonstrated courage to empower others, and had no problem leading the other sailors in a protest.

The book describes a period in American history when Blacks faced prejudice and racism. Blacks wanted better job opportunities, housing, and education. For many Black men during this time, the military was a life-line. It was a way to survive. One of the reasons the black sailors joined the Navy was because it was a path toward a better life. They were able to learn professional skills and earn money to provide for themselves and their families.

This book taught me a lot about the patriotic spirit of Black Americans and how difficult it was being a Black sailor in the Navy during this period.

The Port Chicago 50 were brave to fight for our country and risk their lives, but they were also fighting for their dignity, which is beyond brave.

CHAPTER 2 : BIOGRAPHIES

Biographies are stories told about the lives of people we may or may not be familiar with—historical figures, artists, scientists, entertainers, authors, and more! From well-known people to hidden stories I've never heard of, biographies interest me because it is a way to learn about someone new and how they have contributed to this world we live in. Take a dive in and see what some of my favorite biographies are!

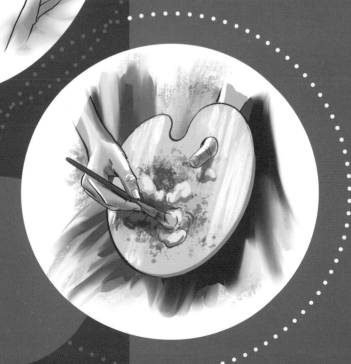

OTHER BOOKS FOR BROS BY
ARNOLD ADOFF

Black is Brown is Tan
I Am the Darker Brother
An Anthology of Modern
Poems by African Americans

Roots and Blues
A Celebration

MALCOLM X

Written by **ARNOLD ADOFF**
Illustrated by **RUDY GUTIERREZ**

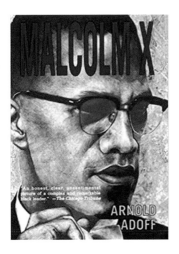

February of each year is normally when we learn about Black history, since it's Black History Month, right? Every year in elementary school, it would seem that we'd always highlight the same individuals: Martin Luther King Jr., Rosa Parks, and Harriet Tubman. All of those people are great, but there are so many legendary people to highlight in history, and February isn't a long enough month to highlight everyone. It also seems that because some had a different approach to activism, they got a bad reputation.

Take Malcolm X, for example, an important leader of Black people in the United States during the civil rights movement. I don't remember ever learning about Malcolm X in any Black history lessons. In fact, my mom told me she experienced the same. She learned more about Martin Luther King Jr. and all the positive accomplishments of his. My mom also mentioned that when reading write-ups and books about Malcolm X, his image was painted as if he was a troublemaker more than a peacemaker.

Thankfully, I found out about the book *Malcolm X* by Arnold Adoff. This is a short book about Malcolm X, from his childhood until he became the activist everyone knows him as. I will warn you that the book does start off kind of heavy. Most know that Malcolm X experienced several personal attacks, as have other activists. The book begins with what he experienced as a Black child growing up in America during a time of segregation and extreme racism.

Although the book is inspiring because it allows us to experience Malcolm X in a powerful, positive light, he got into trouble when he was younger because of personal hardships he experienced. The book also tells us other things that Malcolm X experienced as a child that had an intense impact on him as an adult. Some of the impact was good, and some was not so good. And although he also died a violent death, his ideas still affect people of all races. I'll leave it up to you to read it for yourself.

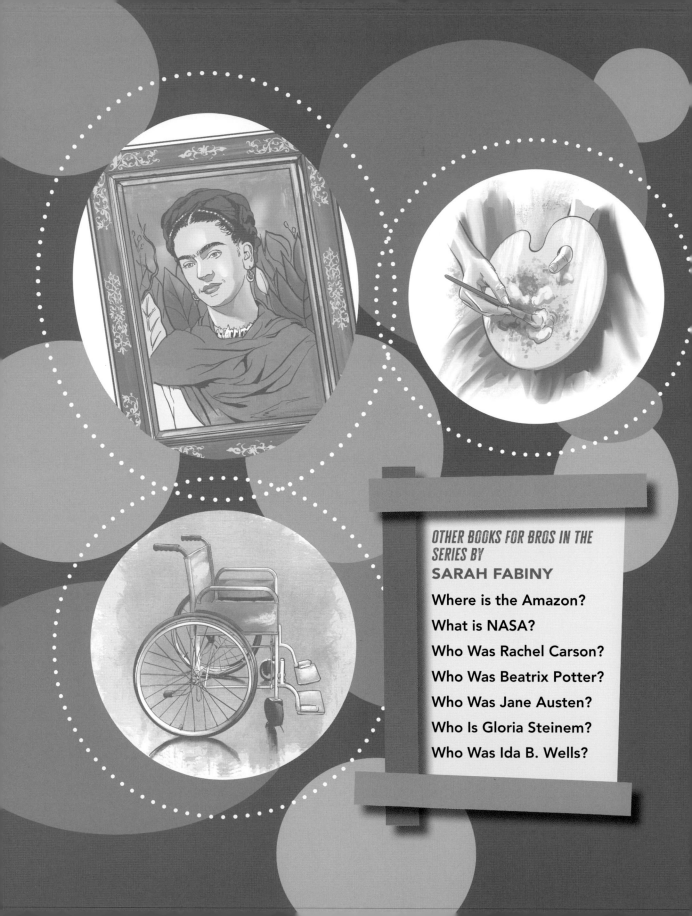

WHO WAS FRIDA KAHLO?

Written by **SARAH FABINY**
Illustrated by **JERRY HOARE**

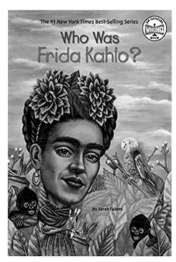

Frida Kahlo was a strong, courageous, and talented Mexican artist who expressed herself through her paintings. She was a self-taught artist who became famous for her self-portraits in particular. I amplify this book about Frida Kahlo because she was an amazing painter, and she was able to break barriers to become world-famous in a male-dominated career.

Because my book club is for boys, I always think it's important for us to acknowledge the important work that girls and women contribute to the world as well. For the last couple of years, we have made it a point to celebrate Women's History Month by reading books that honor powerful women.

Who Was Frida Kahlo? perfectly fit what we needed to celebrate a woman of power as she is someone who beat all odds while maintaining a deep love of her culture. It covers Kahlo's early years growing up in Mexico all the way to her last days. It is known that Frida battled with health issues, and suffered a major accident. Though she experienced hardship and pain, she still created amazing work people appreciate around the world.

In addition to Kahlo being a woman we wanted to celebrate, we also know that we have a diverse group of Bros in our book club. So, honoring a person of color who identified as Mexican has allowed us to use our book club as a platform to bring many more powerful people of color to the surface.

FUN FACT

In 2010, the Mexican government decided to put Frida Kahlo's face on the 500 peso note. Now that's money!

HIDDEN FIGURES
Young Readers' Edition

Written by **MARGOT LEE SHETTERLY**

In 2016, *Hidden Figures* the film was released in theaters and I had no idea how much my perspective would change about women in NASA (the National Aeronautics and Space Administration) by learning about this amazing true story of four African American female mathematicians who helped achieve some of the great moments in our space program during the twentieth century. This was during a time when women did not have the same opportunities as men, and Black people were facing segregation in all areas of society. Before seeing the film, I didn't consider African American women to be such an impactful part of NASA's history. It is hard to believe something is possible if you don't see it. And that's why I'm grateful to the creators of this film and also the book!

As my book club was only a few months old, I was very excited to experience this film with my local Bros. I was even more excited to find out about the book and that there is a young readers' edition for us to enjoy the story even more. And I know what you may

be thinking, should you skip the book if you've seen the movie? Or should you skip the movie if you've read the book already? I say you should never avoid the book when there's a movie of it. In my opinion, the book's always better. With a book, there's more opportunity to see yourself in the story, and more room for imagination.

When watching a movie, your viewpoint is highly influenced by what you see on the screen. I will say that watching *Hidden Figures*, the movie, affected me emotionally because seeing Black women work so hard made me think of my mom, my grandmother, and other hard-working women in my life who don't get enough credit.

In this book, you will learn why these women were known as human computers. When I think of computers, I see laptops, desktops, and PCs, not humans. But these women who were the masterminds behind some of NASA's success were legendary figures—Dorothy Vaughan, Mary Jackson, Katherine Johnson, and Christine Darden. They all were originally working as math teachers in segregated schools but had a life-changing experience working with NASA.

Another amazing feature of this book is reading about people who look like me and members of my family working and enjoying STEM (Science, Technology, Engineering, and Math) careers. This is empowering because it helps us see ourselves doing things that we may have never considered, like working for NASA or becoming a chemist.

Thanks to these four mathematicians, and more women who stepped up to the task, they helped America achieve victory over the Soviet Union during the Cold War. Can you imagine someone who was your math teacher achieving such a high honor? Who are the hidden figures in your life? I am happy that Margot Lee Shetterly brought this story to the world's attention and that these amazing women are no longer hidden.

FUN FACT

Margot Lee Shetterly founded The Human Computer Project, an initiative to reveal all of the women worked as human computers, mathematicians, scientists, and engineers at NACA and NASA between the 1930s and 1980s.

WHO IS MICHAEL JORDAN?

Written by **KIRSTEN ANDERSON** Illustrated by **DEDE PUTRA**

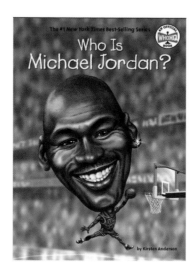

Michael Jordan is considered by many to be the greatest basketball player of all time. He changed the game for the NBA with his natural scoring and jumping abilities. But Jordan's success was not always easy, nor did it happen overnight.

In *Who Is Michael Jordan*, author Kirsten Anderson takes us through MJ's life and career, describing his highest of highs and low points which became the motivation for his success. Surprisingly, he didn't get picked to be on the varsity basketball team his freshman year of high school because he was too short. But over the summer he grew to 6'3. After that, he made the varsity team after playing junior varsity for a year. It was then that he began to receive media attention for his talents. One of the early lessons that you read about is that Jordan was patient and good things happened as a result.

In some ways, I can relate to parts of Jordan's story. When I first started a book club for boys to solely amplify African American literature, it was not always easy. There were tough times

as my mother was raising me as a single parent. I have been turned down for opportunities. And at first, it was difficult finding boys who wanted to read. I wanted to give up because I didn't feel supported. But my mom coached me and pushed me to stay the course. When I listened to her, shortly after I received support like never before. The book club went from 5-6 members to 50 members, then 100, then over 300 at one time! In a blink, your life can change. And like Michael Jordan, I kept believing in myself and pushing through the hard times.

Jordan went on to play college basketball at the University of North Carolina and won an NCAA championship his freshman year. After his junior year in 1984, he was drafted by the Chicago Bulls. Remember what I said about patience? He didn't win an NBA championship until 1991, seven years after being drafted. But shortly after, he won an Olympic gold medal with the Dream Team! Throughout his career, MJ won six NBA championships and never once lost a championship series.

After a turn of events, in 2000, MJ became president of the basketball operations and part-owner of The Washington Wizards basketball team. He was later fired, which was the first time he'd gotten fired by anyone. But he didn't give up. Sound familiar?

He then joined the Charlotte Bobcats as part-owner and president of the basketball operations. A few years later he bought Robert Johnson's share of the Bobcats (now the Charlotte Hornets) and became the first former NBA player to solely own a team! Around this time, MJ is named the highest-paid athlete of all time, and he earned over 100 million dollars on his Nike deal alone! To make even more history, in 2016 he received the Presidential Medal of Freedom from President Barack Obama.

This book is a great way to learn about one of the most iconic figures in sports and business. It shows us why Michael Jordan is an inspiration for so many people.

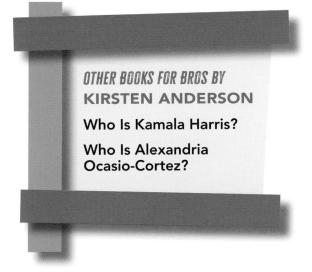

OTHER BOOKS FOR BROS BY
KIRSTEN ANDERSON

Who Is Kamala Harris?

Who Is Alexandria Ocasio-Cortez?

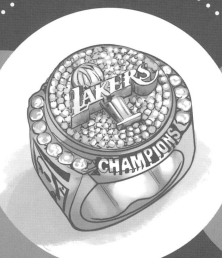

WHO WAS KOBE BRYANT?

Written by **ELLEN LABRECQUE**   Illustrated by **GREGORY COPELAND**

Growing up, I have always been into sports. From swimming, t-ball, basketball, soccer, track, and football, my mom allowed me to try my hand at just about any sport that I wanted. I can only imagine what it's like being as talented as Kobe Bryant though.

It's not surprising someone would write a book about the great Kobe Bryant. He had achieved so much in his short time on earth. He was drafted into the NBA at just seventeen years old and the first of his position to go from high school to the pros. Bryant played for the Los Angeles Lakers for his entire professional basketball career. As a Laker, he became one of the greatest NBA players of all time, winning five NBA championships.

There are so many other notable moments that are described in the book. I was fascinated to learn that Bryant played basketball in Italy before the NBA.

But there is one moment in his career that shocked me. Did you know that thirteen teams passed on signing Bryant during his first draft pick in 1997? Thirteen teams. That's crazy. Kobe Bryant was insanely competitive so

being picked at thirteen only lit a fire beneath him to be even better than what anyone could have imagined.

But he never stopped at basketball. He was a loving husband and father to four girls. And, in fact, Bryant and I have something in common! We both have advocated for diverse African American literature! After Kobe retired, he created a young adult book series called The Wizenard Series, a collection of novels about a young basketball player and his trials to become the best basketball player he can be. He also ran his own entertainment production company called Granity Studios. One day I also hope to be a serial entrepreneur like Kobe was.

To make my dreams a reality, I will just remain confident and disciplined like he was. No matter what, he trusted himself and knew where he needed to be. That's the Mamba mentality we all should grasp onto.

Who Was Kobe Bryant? is a quick read that's full of interesting facts about one of the greatest basketball players of all time. I'm sure reading about Bryant will inspire you just like it inspired me.

IT'S TREVOR NOAH

Born a Crime (Adapted for Young Readers)

Written by **TREVOR NOAH**

This book tells the story of Trevor Noah, host of *The Daily Show*. We don't watch the news or late-night talk shows a lot in my house, but my mom would sometimes tune in to Trevor Noah's talk show and share some of his funny moments with me.

When looking for a new book to provide to my Bros, I saw that Trevor Noah released *It's Trevor Noah: Born a Crime: Stories from a South African Childhood* adapted for young readers. I was honestly thrown off. Because how could he be born a crime? He's one of the smartest, funniest, and coolest guys I've seen on T.V.! He's nothing like a criminal. That's what I thought before I knew he grew up in South Africa with a Black South African mom and a white European dad at a time when interracial relationships were illegal in that country. Apartheid to be specific. I didn't even know what apartheid was before I read this book. One thing Noah explains is that apartheid is a system of racial segregation and it was against the law to be born mixed. When I opened his book and learned this, I was mind blown.

I have never been to South Africa, but after reading this book, I felt like I was there. Noah takes you to his hometown of Johannesburg, one of the biggest cities in South Africa. He talks about the people, the culture, the food, and life in generally. Truly there is no better tour guide than Trevor Noah. He makes reading informative but light and funny at times. You can hear his voice in your head as you're reading. As a writer myself, I know that is not an easy thing to do.

The book is dedicated to his mom and it is obvious that she is his hero. He talks about how she raised and instilled him with values like being an independent thinker. And reading this book you're holding right now, you can probably tell that my mom is my hero too. Reading how fearless his mom was, how she marched to the beat of her own drum, and just how rebellious she was, reminds me of my mom raising me.

It's Trevor Noah is truly one of my favorite books. I'm glad he made a kid-

IN THE MEDIA

I've been raised by a woman who's been a blogger and full-time entrepreneur. My grandmother has been a radio host, journalist, script writer for news anchors, and familiar with pretty much everything in the media. Even my uncle Ishmael is a journalist and a couple of my great uncles work in radio. Watching all these family members work in the media has inspired me to one day try it out as well!

friendly version so that me and other Bros could read. His childhood story gives hope to people. Reading it made me more grateful for all the hard work that was put into raising me and for all of the amazing opportunities I have had, which I never could have imagined.

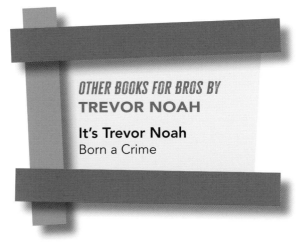

OTHER BOOKS FOR BROS BY TREVOR NOAH

It's Trevor Noah
Born a Crime

THE FAIRMOUN...

VOL. 1, NO. 87

Race Hate invades State

KU KLUX KLAN IN 60 INDIANA

Break Seen In Miners' Pay Dispute

BLACK BOY

Written by **RICHARD WRIGHT**

I was introduced to Richard Wright's *Black Boy* in 2021, It's considered one of the most important books about Black life written by an African American. My mom said that she wanted to make sure I read this book before I went to college.

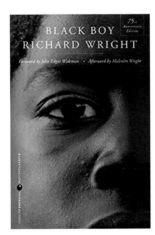

In *Black Boy*, Richard Wrights tells his story of growing up in poverty in the South. He lived in Memphis, Tennessee, and different parts of Arkansas and Mississippi. The story takes place between 1912 and 1937 when Blacks were living under a code of laws called Jim Crow. This meant that opportunities for Blacks were limited and living conditions were harsh.

Throughout the book, Richard Wright describes how he would get into trouble as a young boy trying to feed himself or to stay away from people who were harming him. Although he admits he was mischievous, Richard Wright had a strong desire to read and learn. I guess you can say he was a natural when it came to school. I kind of think of him as a Bro before the Bros.

The book also describes his leaving the hardships of the South to move to Chicago where he established his writing career. For better opportunities, many other Blacks during Richard Wright's time moved out of the South to places up north like Chicago, Detroit, and other cities on the East Coast. This was called the Great Migration.

One of the big messages Richard Wright expresses in this book is that Black people haven't always had access to literacy. We weren't allowed to know how to read for a long time. That's how I know it is so important for me to continue the mission of Books N Bros and advocating for African American literacy.

To this day there are still many people who don't have access to public libraries or books at all, for that matter. Although Wright's *Black Boy* caused a lot of uproar back in the 1940s when it was published, I am grateful that he had the confidence to use his voice.

CHAPTER 3

NOVELS, SHORT STORIES & POEMS

My mom noticed my love of reading when I was young. Since then novels, short stories, and poems have become some of my personal favorites.

For example, I was introduced to *Clayton Byrd Goes Underground* when I was only eleven years old. Then I learned of *All American Boys*, *The Hate U Give*, and more! They're easy to follow. Some may be more emotional to read, but that's between you and the pages of the book. If you can't figure out which books are best for you, I recommend giving any of these next options a try. Especially if you are looking for African American literature.

Stories are told right from our own experiences and from those closest to us. The books I'm sharing here are books about history that I never knew I needed but when I read them, I was excited to share them with my Bros and now with you too!

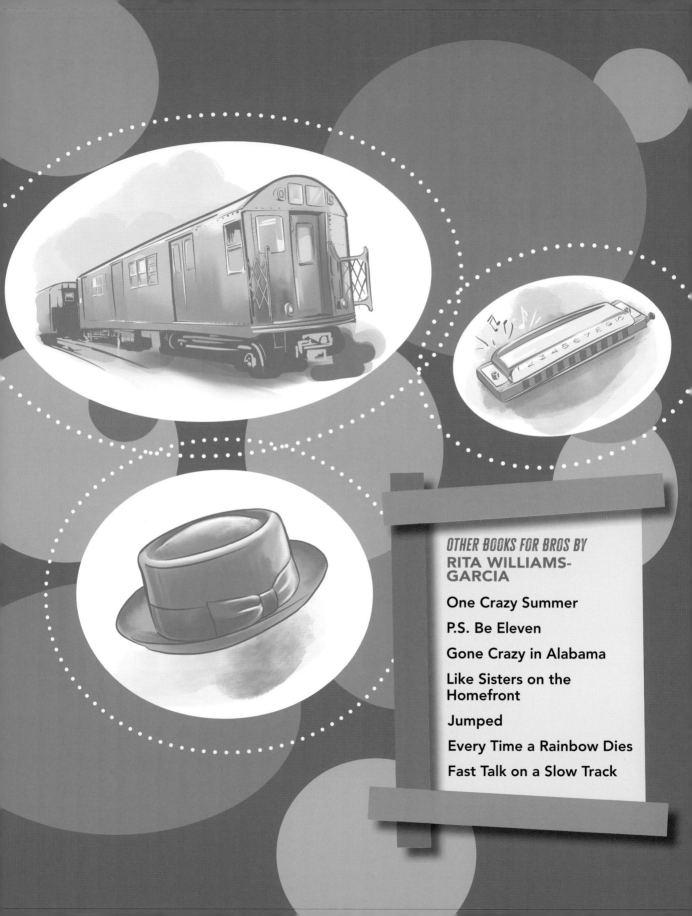

CLAYTON BYRD GOES UNDERGROUND

Written by **RITA WILLIAMS-GARCIA**

June 10, 2017 was the first time I traveled to New York. Why is this important? Because my team and I had a meet and greet with people of the Brooklyn community and we were surprised to meet Rita Williams-Garcia! She is a *New York Times* bestselling author and Newbery honor author.

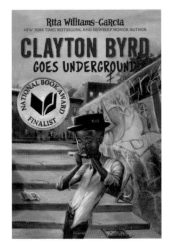

In *Clayton Byrd Goes Underground,* the character of Clayton loves to play music with his grandfather, Cool Papa Byrd. But when Cool Papa Byrd dies, Clayton's mother forbids him to play the blues, so he runs away, and his adventure begins. When we first picked up *Clayton Byrd Goes Underground,* it made my mom think of my relationship with my grandpa. We'd always sing songs together when I was small. I liked old-school music and some current stuff. But in *Clayton Byrd Goes Underground,* Cool Papa Byrd was way more into the blues than my grandpa.

In an interview, Rita Williams-Garcia mentioned that her husband, a musician helped her to understand musical terms and how a band plays together. She also purchased a harmonica (also known as the blues harp) and learned to play it. The research she did for this book paid off because it felt special and authentic.

If you're interested in music, its history, and fascinating people, this one is for you. It also includes unexpected adventures.

This story so relatable, especially if you have ever had a close relationship with your grandparent or a family member who influenced you in some major way. And Clayton Byrd's grandpa influenced him and his love for blues music.

Clayton Byrd Goes Underground is a realistic story of loss, family, and love that many people will relate to. It's also a cool way to learn about music, especially the blues.

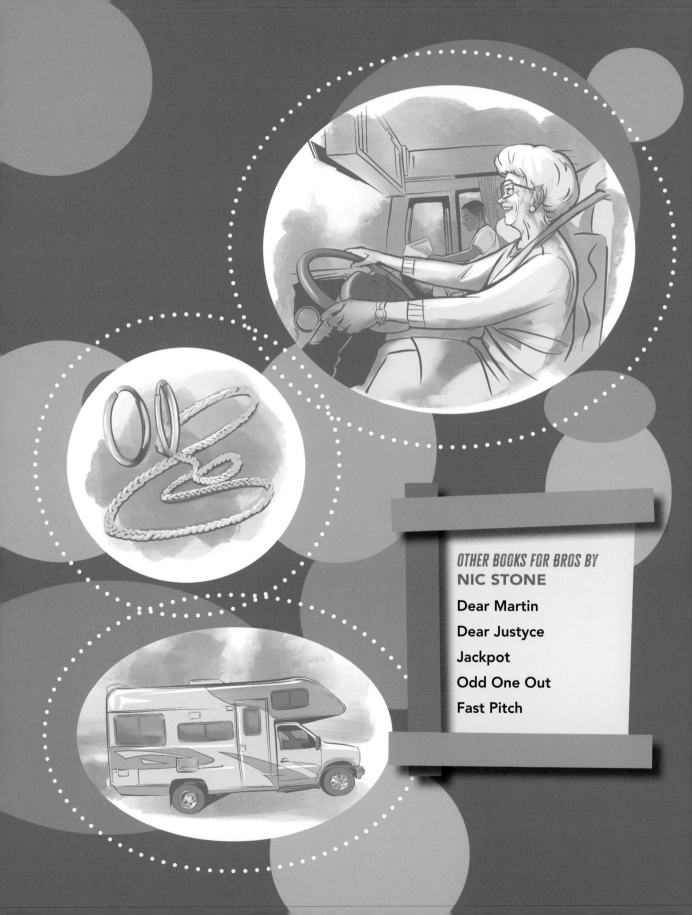

OTHER BOOKS FOR BROS BY
NIC STONE

Dear Martin

Dear Justyce

Jackpot

Odd One Out

Fast Pitch

CLEAN GETAWAY

Written by **NIC STONE**

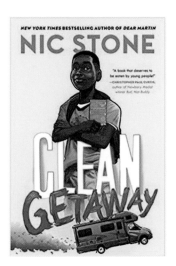

If your grandmother is one of your favorite people on Earth then you will absolutely enjoy reading *Clean Getaway*. It's about Scoob, a teenage boy, traveling on a road trip with his grandma through the American South, learning about its past and its present through landmarks of the civil rights movement and what they mean to us today. It's not your typical adventure novel, especially with a grandma as a main character—she has her own mysteries going on.

One of the features about this book that makes it relatable is that we meet Scoob as he is dealing with real issues. He gets in trouble when protecting a friend from a bully. This upsets his father and Scoob gets grounded. As you can guess, he is excited to get away with his grandma to escape his troubles at home and school.

As you follow Scoob and his grandma on their adventure, you get to learn about events and people such as Medgar Evers and Emmitt Till who were important to the civil rights movement. Before reading this book, I wasn't aware of *The Negro Travelers' Green Book*. Scoob, the main character, hears about this guide from his grandma and quickly understands that their trip is going to be a memorable experience. During the era of segregation in the American South, "Green Book" was used to show Black travelers where to dine, find lodging, and avoid racist encounters. This was a real guide, folks. And obviously, this opened up the opportunity to talk about that more with my mom.

There is so much to love about this book. You've got the grandmother and grandson relationship, a car ride through the American South, interesting facts about history, drama between a father and son, and exciting and suspenseful moments throughout. Truly, it's all there for you in this enjoyable read.

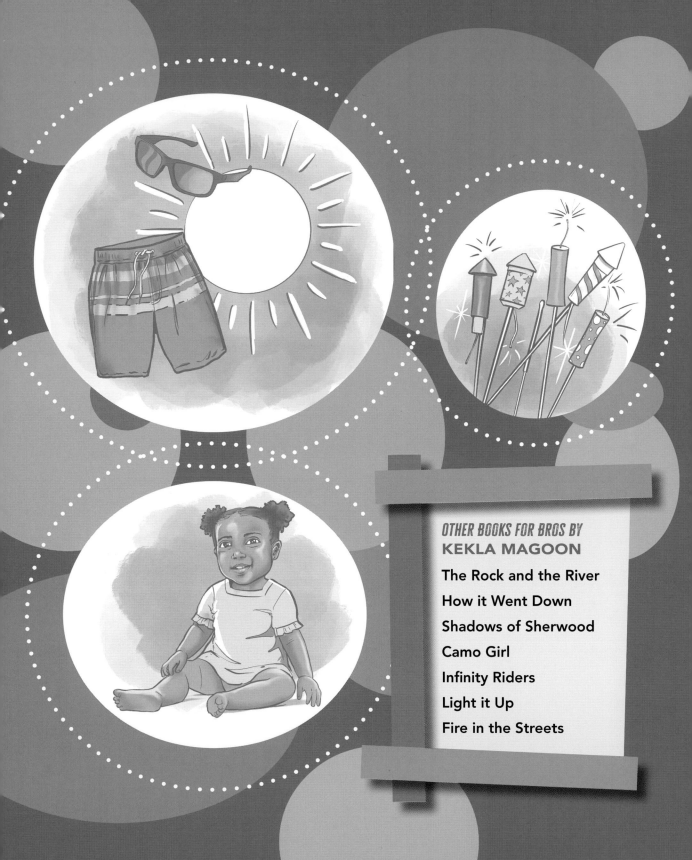

OTHER BOOKS FOR BROS BY
KEKLA MAGOON

The Rock and the River

How it Went Down

Shadows of Sherwood

Camo Girl

Infinity Riders

Light it Up

Fire in the Streets

THE SEASON OF STYX MALONE

Written by **KEKLA MAGOON**

If you're looking for a book full of Black boy joy, magic, and wonder, you will enjoy *The Season of Styx Malone*. This book got my attention because I like stories with adventure.

In this fun story, Caleb Franklin and his brother Bobby Gene have the ultimate adventure when they meet the cool Styx Malone one summer. Styx promises they can pull off the Great Escalator Trade—exchanging one small thing for something better until they achieve their wildest dreams.

But the adventure with Styx is more than what they expected. You have to read the book to find out what it is! Have you ever had a summer you'll never forget? This was one summer Caleb and Bobby Gene would never ever forget.

One of my best friends came to mind when reading this because I would spend time with him and his family when my mom worked long hours. And whenever there was a day or few days that I knew that I was staying the night, that also meant time to explore. These were great times. We would just get lost in fun and adventure.

And this is why we chose this story for the Bros. It's important to see Black

boys having fun, just like Styx, Caleb, and Bobby Gene. This is especially true because Black boys and girls are often seen as older than what they are. We see it this over and over again with how we are disciplined or talked about on TV and social media. And so it's great to have these stories about kids not having to worry about the world making us grow up too fast. It's all about being able to enjoy our childhood and Styx Malone does a really good job at showing Black boys and girls as kids being kids.

FUN FACT

One of Kekla Magoon's favorite books is a classic titled Roll of Thunder, Here Me Cry by Mildred C. Taylor, a historical novel that published in 1973. Both Taylor and Magoon were Coretta Scott King Award honorees.

GHOST Track 1

Written by **JASON REYNOLDS**

After reading *Ghost*, Jason Reynolds became one of my favorite writers. Ghost is about a thirteen-year-old boy, Castle Crenshaw, aka Ghost, who is naturally great at running. He wasn't trained to run track, he didn't attend an elite school where all students were expected to play sports, he simply knew how to run. And Ghost knew how to run FAST. But when he's chosen for an elite middle school track team, he not only has to prove himself on the track, he also has to deal with other problems in his life.

jasonreynolds

NATIONAL BOOK AWARD FINALIST

GHOST

RUNNING FOR HIS LIFE, OR FROM IT?

From the bright yellow book cover to the quick glimpse you catch of a Black boy running off the cover, I was intrigued to see what this book was about. Honestly it's about real life hardship. Ghost has a violent father, and his mom works really hard just to barely make ends meet. Ghost makes decisions that would bring about major consequences for anyone, and like many people, he tries to overshadow and run from his problems. That is why he is so fast on the track. He is literally running for his life, until the coach realizes he has more to offer and a promising future.

This book was chosen for Books N Bros because it just connects with us. There are so many of us Bros who are into other activities like sports or music or art. And just like Ghost, we have to find ways to develop our talents as we deal with real issues in our lives. One of thing this book does well is speak to issues we kids deal with in a language we understand. Ghost talks like we talk, so it's easy see to ourselves in his story.

Another reason this was a perfect book for Books N Bros is because it brings up the importance of having supportive people in your life like friends, coaches, parents, and big Bros. Like Ghost, when we are dealing with problems, it helps to not have to deal with it all on your own. But I won't give too much of the story away.

If you or someone you know is into sports, I would recommend this book. It's not your stereotypical sports book. It inspires you to look at people for who they are, who they can be. And it even looks at how you can improve yourself. I really appreciate Jason Reynolds for this one and the many moments of wisdom it shares.

THE STARS BENEATH OUR FEET

Written by **DAVID BARCLAY MOORE**

This novel is the story of a boy, Lolly Rachpaul, who's grieving the loss of his brother, Jermaine, in a gang-related shooting. He's living in the projects of Harlem with his mother. In addition to having a hard time understanding his brother's death, his parents are also divorced, he's dealing with peer pressure, and he has other challenges.

The thing that most offers him a sense of peace is building with the huge amount of Legos his mother's girlfriend gives him for Christmas.

When the book club read this book, we weren't reading heavy emotional titles but this book does not shy away from serious topics. One thing that sparked a deep conversation was Lolly feeling grief after the death of his brother. I appreciate David Barclay Moore bringing up this issue because so many of us have to deal with it in our lives. Just reading about how Lolly handles his grief, helps anyone else who may be feeling the same way.

Some other big themes this book covers include family bonds, support for mental health, the power of friendship, following your dreams, and making peace with the past.

We even had a couple of parents thank us for choosing this book because it gave them a way to address hard conversations…but made them easier. No one really wants to talk about death, divorce, or who their parents are dating if they don't have to. But we cannot keep sweeping difficult topics under the rug.

David Barclay Moore was bold for writing for this and it shows. *The Stars Beneath Our Feet* is an amazing novel (which won the Coretta Scott King-John Steptoe Award for New Talent) to address all those hard topics and more.

OTHER BOOKS FOR BROS BY
SHARON G. FLAKE

The Skin I'm In

Money Hungry

Bang!

Who Am I Without Him?

Begging for Change

Pinned

The Broken Bike Boy and
the Queen of 33rd Street

YOU DON'T EVEN KNOW ME

Stories and Poems About Boys

Written by **SHARON G. FLAKE**

You Don't Even Know Me is a collection of stories and poems that provides insight into the minds of a diverse group of adolescent Black boys from a teen perspective as they face challenges in their lives. I describe it as the book that will fulfill the wonder you may have had about what the guy in your class is thinking.

The book begins with a poem titled after the book "You Don't Even Know Me." It sets up the book nicely because it's about a boy who feels he is not being noticed. He believes in himself despite the lack of attention.

From there it goes into short stories and more poems. They all talk about different experiences that young Black boys are having every day. Some of the other poems that stand out include:

• "People Might Not Understand" is about a boy who wants to become the president

• "Sixteen" is a really really short poem about how this one boy views his world

• "Words to the World" is about how much a boy loves his sister

Just like *The Stars Beneath Our Feet,* some of the stories in this book spark intense conversations because they deal with heavy topics. These are a few that stood out to me:

• "Gettin' Even" tells of a young boy who wants revenge for his grandfather's death

• "Infected" is about a boy who has to confront the fact that he may have a life-altering disease

• "Scared to Death" is the story of Tow-Kaye's who is getting married as a teenager to his pregnant girlfriend, the love of his life. This story resonated with my mom, as she became a mother at a young age. Tow-Kaye's experience is just one of the several stories in this book that I believe is a great read for teens, parents of teens, and even educators that work with teens on a daily basis.

Navigating life can be complex but as a teenager, there is so much to learn in what seems like such a short period of time. Thankfully, we have books like *You Don't Even Know Me* to help get through these times.

OTHER BOOKS FOR BROS BY
BRENDAN KIELY

Tradition

The Last True Love Story

The Gospel of Winter

The Other Talk:
Reckoning with Our White
Privilege

ALL AMERICAN BOYS

Written by **JASON REYNOLDS** and **BRENDAN KIELY**

Talk about a powerful book that truly imitates life, a life that Black and Brown people wish didn't exist, the reality that you're seen as a threat to society just because you're a person of color.

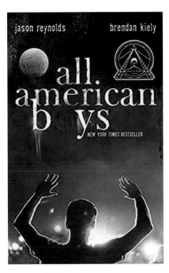

Authors Jason Reynolds and Brendan Kiely said that they wrote *All American Boys* as a response to incidents where young Black boys were harmed or killed due to encounters with police or racial profiling. They felt that the book would start an honest conversation about why these incidents were happening and what we all can do about them.

All American Boys is inspired by real-life events and unveils two layers of the impact of police brutality (and racial attacks in general). Those two layers are the experience of the victim of police brutality, Rashad, a teenage Black boy, and Quinn, a teenage white boy, who's in a tricky position, because he saw what happened. He's Rashad's classmate but also a family friend of the police officer who brutally beat Rashad.

The harsh reality for Black people in America is that we are shown at a young age how to protect ourselves (and even our siblings, cousins, etc.) from racism. We don't get to experience the joy of bike riding to the middle of nowhere and getting lost in nature. We instead have to make sure that our parents know where we are going so we don't end up in places where it's not safe. We have to make sure we are near neighbors who would advocate for us instead of calling themselves neighborhood watch, only to kill us in the middle of the street because our hoodies make them feel unsafe.

While we have this harsh reality, we still have the heart to trust some of the white allies in our space. These are people like author Brendan Kiely who acknowledge that racism affects people of color in harmful ways and they want to do something about it.

All American Boys is a necessary read for understanding race relations in America. I recommend it for any book club like Books N Bros where Black and Brown boys are the primary members.

BOY21

Written by **MATTHEW QUICK**

You may be familiar with the saying, "Misery loves company." Oftentimes when I've used that phrase, it's honestly from an angle of "I don't want to be attached to THAT negativity."

But after reading *Boy21*, I've been reminded that it's natural to bond with someone over trauma. That is the connection shown in *Boy21* between the characters of Russ and Finley, two high school seniors who seem to have nothing in common, but who end up helping each other through pain, competition, basketball, and more.

Like *All American Boys*, *Boy21* is another book about the friendship between a Black boy and a white boy. But it's so different.

Finley is the only white boy on his school's basketball team, and he wears the number 21 jersey. We see him navigate his experience in his community of Bellmont that silences violence, racism, and drug use. We also watch as Finley tries to find balance between basketball and Erin, a girl

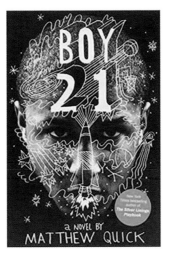

he likes. Then Russ enters the story. He is a Black boy from who is new to Finley's school. He is also a basketball player whose former jersey number was 21. We meet Russ as his life has been turned upside down by tragedy. But Russ only answers to the name of Boy21 and believes he's from outer space.

Finley and Russ become friends and realize they in fact have more in common than their passion for playing basketball. They come from two different worlds. Russ comes from a very affluent community and Finley's town of Bellmont has a history of being trash-filled and violent. But even with their different experiences in life, they become closer. Finley shares a very intimate secret about his mother and Russ shares more about his parents as well.

This was a great book for the Bros because it's all about family, friendship, and the compassion that can exist between two boys from different backgrounds.

FUN FACT

Brian F. Walker not only wanted to highlight issues around representation by writing Black Boy White School, but as an adult, he returned to the prep school of his youth to represent for Black boys, teach, and coach basketball. What a great way to give back.

BLACK BOY WHITE SCHOOL

Written by **BRIAN F. WALKER**

The issue of stereotyping is front and center in the book, and it takes you inside an elite private school but from the perspective of a Black teenage boy.

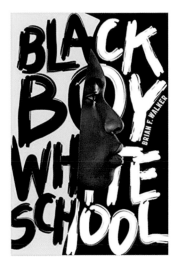

In *Black Boy White School*, Anthony "Ant" "Tony" grew up in East Cleveland and had the traumatic experience of witnessing his friend Mookie killed in a drive-by shooting. After this incident, Anthony is presented with an opportunity to get out of that neighborhood and attend a predominantly white preparatory school in Maine known as Belton Academy, where he has a chance to better himself, but he also has to figure out where he belongs.

After becoming a student at Belton Academy, the white students refuse to call him by his first name, which bothers him. They call him Tony and assume he's from New York and that he likes basketball. But Anthony also makes assumptions about his white classmates.

Like most new kids, he struggles with how to fit in at this new school, of a different class level than he's familiar with. He also realizes that he no longer can directly relate to the kids back home in East Cleveland either. To them, he's changed because he is preppy and acts more like the white kids at his school.

Anthony's experience is one that many Black Americans can relate to. Sometimes we have to exist in spaces like Belton Academy where we are the outsider. Sometimes we don't know if we should follow the crowd or stand alone. Unfortunately, this experience leads some to think that "white is right." As kids, we don't always understand the reasons behind why we might feel this way. Systemic racism such as redlining (government maps outlining where Blacks lived) or gentrification (when a poor urban area is changed by wealthier people moving in) has much to do with it. It creates a "haves" and "have nots" environment and you become envious of those who have.

Black Boy White School takes us on an emotional roller coaster as an intense story about what it means to exist between two different worlds.

THE HATE U GIVE

Written by **ANGIE THOMAS**

This powerful novel hits home, as it was inspired by the Black Lives Matter movement and born after the unrest in Ferguson, Missouri following the murder of Mike Brown—who was killed by Officer Darren Wilson—and other Black individuals who lost their lives at the hands of police.

At the time of the Michael Brown incident, we lived ten minutes away from Ferguson. We drove through Ferguson regularly and we still have family and friends who live in that area. I never imagined the small municipality of Ferguson would hit the international media as it did after Mike Brown's death.

The injustice that occurred in Ferguson lit a fire beneath creators and writers alike. In *The Hate U Give*, author Angie Thomas introduces us to Starr, a 16-year-old Black teen who witnesses the murder of her unarmed friend, Khalil. Starr is also navigating the reality of many Black students who live in poor, neglected areas but attend school in more affluent neighborhoods.

Starr is challenged with how to properly grieve her friend, while navigating in an environment that is the polar opposite of where she lives (think *Black Boy White School*). Additionally, activism chooses her as she decides to advocate for what's right and her life takes a major shift. Oddly enough, this is the reality for many of us, as we were all trying to process the murder of an innocent Black teen, by an officer who was supposed to only serve and protect. August 9, 2014 changed a lot of lives, and sadly Mike Brown had to lose his in order for others to see what they needed to really live for.

When creating Starr and the other children in the book, Angie Thomas said that she wanted to treat them as roses growing from concrete. This idea was inspired by the late actor and music artist Tupac who also inspired the book's title.

In 2018, *The Hate U Give* was released as a major motion picture starring Amandla Stenberg, Issa Rae, and Common, among other talented actors. The one thing that both the book and the movie do well is show

how tragic encounters between the police and communities of color affect everyday people.

When *The Hate U Give* was released it took off like a wildfire winning numerous awards and honors. Read the book and you'll know why. This was just the book we needed during a difficult time. We Bros are grateful for Angie Thomas for writing it.

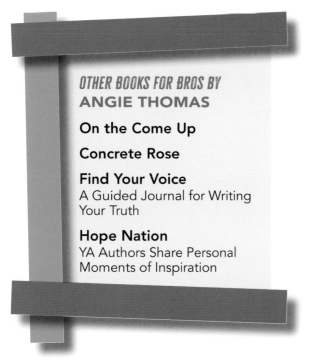

OTHER BOOKS FOR BROS BY ANGIE THOMAS

On the Come Up

Concrete Rose

Find Your Voice
A Guided Journal for Writing Your Truth

Hope Nation
YA Authors Share Personal Moments of Inspiration

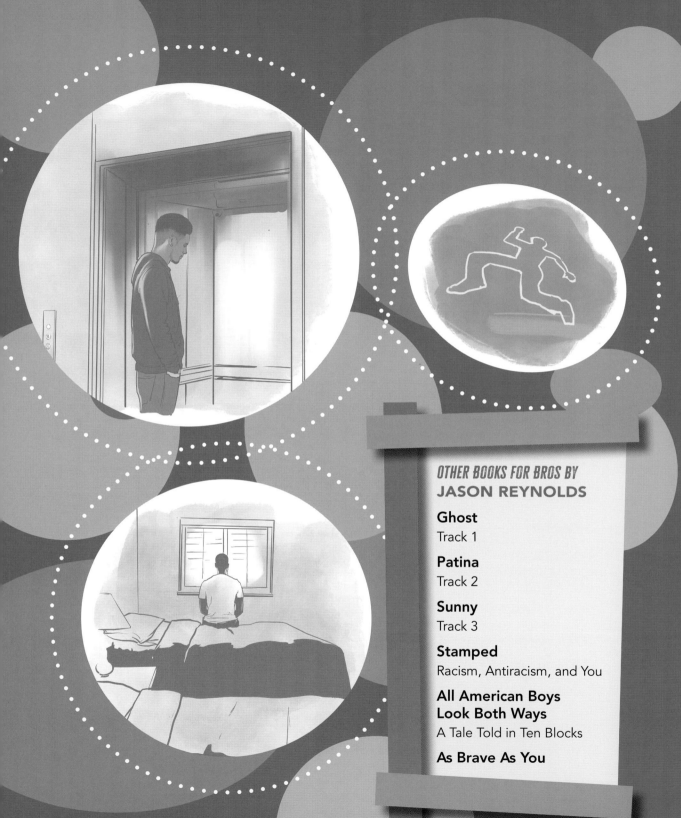

LONG WAY DOWN

Written by **JASON REYNOLDS**

The Long Way Down by Jason Reynolds is personally one of my favorite books. It is set in an elevator and the entire story lasts 68 seconds. It's a very gritty and emotional book that centers around the main character Will whose big brother Shawn was shot and killed due to gang crime. And it captures the time it takes Will to decide whether or not he's going to avenge his brother's death. As Will gets on the elevator, he knows who he's after. But as it stops on each floor, someone connected to his brother gets on to give Will a different piece of a bigger story than what he thinks he already knows.

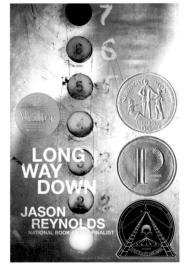

The book goes step-by-step through how Will deals with his grief and his journey for revenge. I give credit to Jason Reynolds for writing about such a difficult topic to discuss. The emotions Will deals with on that elevator—anger, trauma, sadness, grief, guilt—are familiar to all of us. And I know that Will and Shawn's story is relatable to many of us who live in or near communities where violence is normalized. So this is a book that helps you identify your emotions and deal with them before making big decisions.

The story is written in free verse and organized creatively on the page, which actually adds more character to each word. I also appreciate the tension that is created by Jason Reynolds. It's like you can't wait to get to the next page to see what Will is going to do or what piece of the story he's going to receive next.

The Long Way Down is a must-read for middle school and high school students because it sparks spirited discussions about friends, feelings, and life in general.

FUN FACT

Aside from being a great writer, Jason Reynolds is also a poet. His first book was a book of poetry which he sold out of the trunk of his car. Now that's hustling.

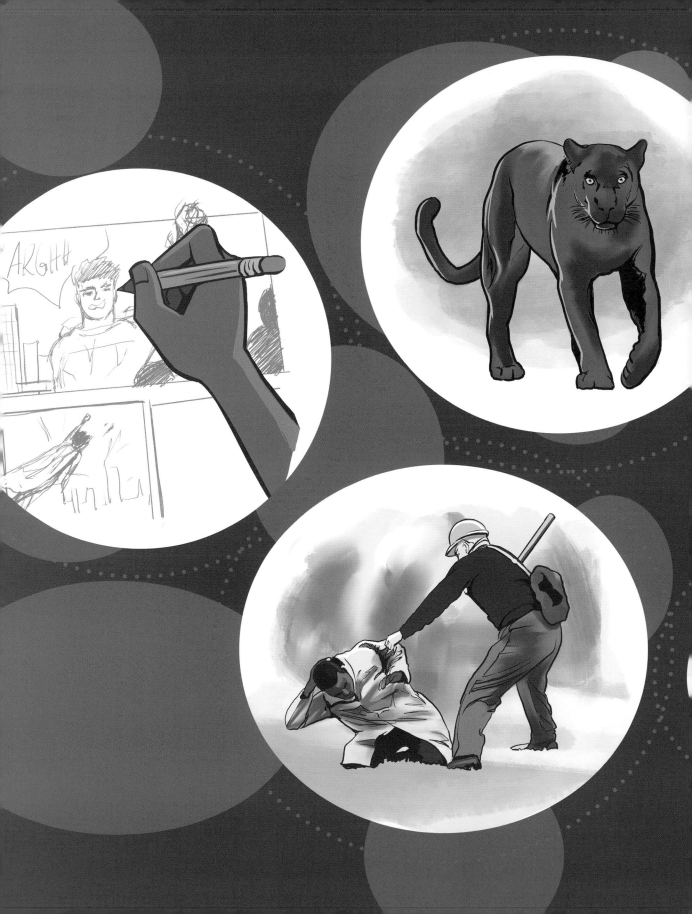

CHAPTER 4 : COMICS, GRAPHIC NOVELS, SUPERHEROES & SCIENCE FICTION

Superhero here! The Spectacular Sidney (if you know you know). Graphic novels, comics, superheroes, and science fiction have always been favorites among the book club. I grew up with a love of graphic novels and comics such as *Diary of a Wimpy Kid*, *Black Panther*, and more. My mom and I both believe that graphic novels are for kids ages two to 102. They expand the imagination by seeing the characters illustrated, and at certain moments being able to illustrate them ourselves in our imagination when there are no graphics.

And we all love superheroes, right? Unless you're some secret villain or hero-hating, world-destroying mastermind, your answer should be yes! Although something a lot of Black kids struggle with is seeing heroes who look like them. Diversity in the superhero universe has gotten better over time. We just need to continue to push for representation in movies, comics, and more! It's necessary for us kids to be able to see ourselves as the good guys in a story with characters who we can relate to on a personal level.

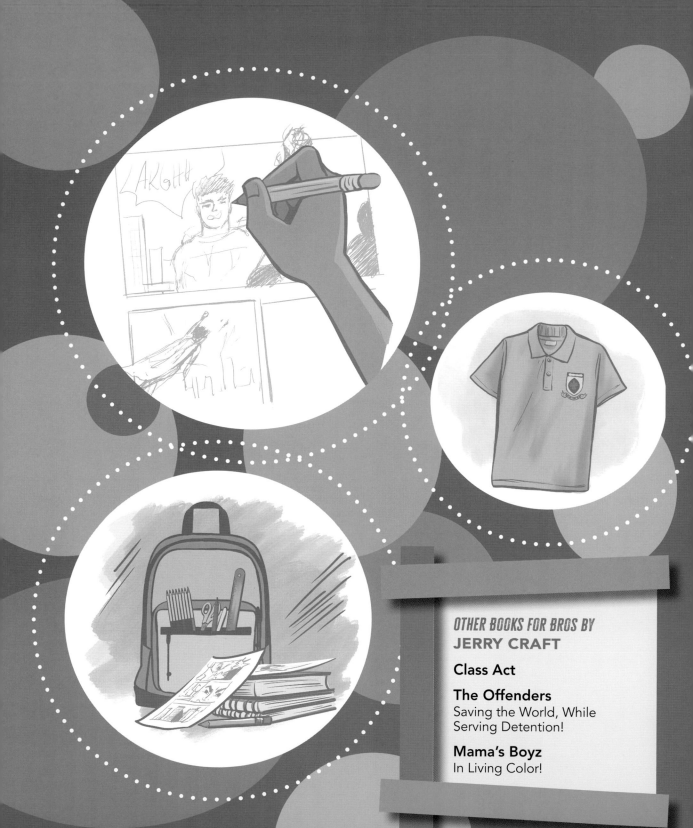

OTHER BOOKS FOR BROS BY JERRY CRAFT

Class Act

The Offenders
Saving the World, While Serving Detention!

Mama's Boyz
In Living Color!

NEW KID

Written by **JERRY CRAFT**

This is one of my favorite graphic novels. As a Black boy who's navigated the public school system and then shifted to attending private schools, reading *New Kid* gave me a vivid perspective on starting over at a new school and the struggle to fit in.

I enjoyed reading *New Kid* book in the book club with my Bros as we escaped inside Jordan's journey as the new kid at a private school where he's one of the few kids of color in his grade. Jordan is not thrilled about going to this school but his mom is so excited about the opportunity because she feels it is safer than his neighborhood public school and she associates the private school with success.

At first, Jordan struggles to adjust, and feels as if he is maneuvering in a space full of micro and macro aggressions that feel racially motivated. But Jordan is a talented cartoon artist. In fact, he would have rather gone to an art school than a fancy prep school. He uses his art as a way to escape some uncomfortable experiences at school.

Jordan also makes a few friends that help him get through his first year.

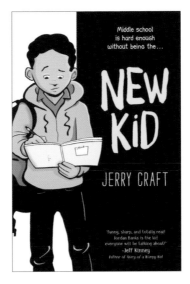

There is Liam, a white kid who was designated to help Jordan adjust to the new school. Drew and Jordan bond over their similar interests and the fact that they both come from disadvantaged neighborhoods. And there is Alexandra, who is insecure about a scar on her arm. Like Jordan, each of his friends has their own issue that they must confront throughout the school year.

Jerry Craft is both the author and illustrator of *New Kid*. The Bros and I agree, he did a beautiful job of taking us through the mind of a teen experiencing a big life change in a colorful, whimsical yet heart-tugging way.

FUN FACT

Jerry Craft's book *The Offenders: Saving the World, while Serving Detention* was co-written by his two sons, Aren and Jaylen. For their work toward literacy, I consider Aren and Jaylen honorary Bros.

MORE BOOKS FOR BROS BY
DAVID K. GORDEN

**Kwame Hightower and
the Man With No Name**
Hardcover: Deluxe Edition

**Kwame Hightower and
the New Knights**
Adventure Coloring Book

KWAME HIGHTOWER
And the Man with No Name

Written by **DAVID K. GORDEN**

As a St. Louis native, I never imagined what it would look like for a family to relocate from St. Louis to a place outside of the United States. That is until we chose this book as a book club read for the Bros.

In the book, we are introduced to twelve-year-old Kwame—who is just your average kid—as he adapts to living in London, England. Kwame misses his old home and really doesn't like living in this new country, so his mom takes him to Buckingham Palace in London where the Queen and the royal family lives. She hopes it will help him warm up to his new environment. It is there that he has another life-changing experience. He pulls the legendary sword Excalibur from the sacred stone, making him the king of England!

Little does he know that this is only the beginning of an adventure in which

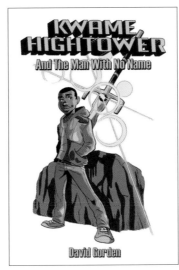

he must come to grips with his role and powers to unravel a deadly conspiracy.

At the heart of Kwame's character is his desire to stick up for what's right. Yet simultaneously, there's a larger situation at hand that neither Kwame nor his mother know about until life changes for the both of them forever.

We St. Louis natives are proud of David K. Gorden because *Kwame Hightower: And the Man With No Name* is a special treat for middle and high-school-aged readers.

FUN FACT

David K. Gorden is a creator from St. Louis, who fell in love with art and storytelling at a young age, making his own comics and submitting them to the local newspaper at eight years old!

MARCH

Written by **JOHN LEWIS** and **ANDREW AYDIN**
Illustrated by **NATE POWELL**

The *March* series of three graphic-novel memoirs vividly illustrates the challenges and triumphs of the civil rights movement through the eyes of former United States Congressman John Lewis, an American hero who fought for equality for more than fifty years.

Each book covers different parts of John Lewis' life and the challenges and triumphs he faced fighting for civil rights.

In Book One, we meet a proud John Lewis as he is preparing to attend the inauguration ceremony of Barack Obama, the first African American president of the United States. The book then dives into Lewis' early years in rural Georgia as the son of a sharecropper who is committed to getting an education by any means. When he is rejected by a predominantly-white college, he attends a theological school where he becomes active in organizing non-violent protests against segregation and soon meets civil rights hero Dr. Martin Luther King Jr. This book shows us the roots of John Lewis' activism which would become his life's work.

Book Two begins with John Lewis watching Barack Obama become sworn in as the 44th president of the United States. A comparison is made between Obama's inauguration speech and Lewis' speech when he was elected as chairman of the Student Nonviolent Coordinating Committee (SNCC). The book goes on to show how Lewis and other activists organized Freedom Rides throughout the South. These were protests where individuals of different races would ride buses to protest local segregation laws. We also see Lewis play a role in the famous 1963 March on Washington where Martin Luther King, Jr. gave his famous "I Have a Dream" speech. Lewis also gave a powerful speech that day.

Book Three takes readers on an emotional rollercoaster as John Lewis recounts some of the highs and lows he encountered throughout his life as a civil rights leader. Lewis is heartbroken by the news of the bombing of the Sixteenth Street Baptist Church in Birmingham, Alabama where four young girls were killed in a racist attack. This event, along with the assassinations of Malcolm X and President John F. Kennedy Jr., reminds Lewis that the fight for freedom must remain steadfast. Then we see a few high points as civil rights leaders celebrate the passing of the 1964 Civil Rights Act which prohibited discrimination based on race, color, religion, sex, or national origin, and the 1965 Voting Rights Act which ensured Blacks and other races had a right to vote.

In addition to following Lewis' journey, the *March* series is a blueprint for young and aspiring activists to use. We often say history repeats itself. Unfortunately, we are still fighting racism in various forms today. With this series, we're able to see the value in determination, organized activism, and how to find one's voice after seeing how someone like Lewis' good trouble paid off.

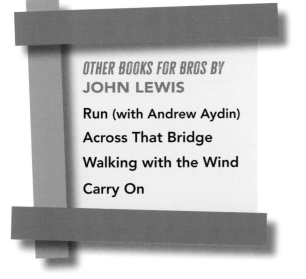

OTHER BOOKS FOR BROS BY JOHN LEWIS

Run (with Andrew Aydin)

Across That Bridge

Walking with the Wind

Carry On

OTHER BOOKS FOR BROS BY TY ALLAN JACKSON

The Supadupa Kid 2

Danny Dollar Millionaire Extraordinaire
The Lemonade Escapade

Make Your Own Money
How Kids Can Earn It, Save It, Spend It and Dream Big

You Are Amazing, I Am Amazing

When I Close My Eyes

THE SUPADUPA KID

Written by **TY ALLAN JACKSON**
Illustrated by **JONATHAN SHEARS**

The Supadupa Kid combines not only representations of diverse skin color into a superhero book but also relatable ages and personalities. The main character, Javon Williams, is a good-hearted, normal kid who is very adamant about his sneaker collection, listening to music, playing baseball, and as a teenager, he's also interested in his crush from school.

Because every superhero story needs a villain, in this one, we have Hoody. Unfortunately for Javon, Hoody is the neighborhood bully and he just loves to be mean. Javon and Hoody encounter each other on a rainy day and both are struck by lightning. The lightning strike gives Javon superpowers and he becomes *The Supadupa Kid*, the city's hero.

Other memorable characters include Ronald, Supadupa Kid's best friend and assistant, who is actually a genius, and then there's Javon's tattle-tale sisters who annoy our superhero, but they are funny.

Of course, when you have two opposing forces with superpowers, there is bound to be a clash. I won't give the story away, but there is an exciting ending to this story.

While reading *The Supadupa Kid,* I was able to see myself in the main character's shoes with my best friend at my side which made reading it so much more enjoyable.

Ty Allan Jackson's imagination soars in this book just like The Supadupa Kid himself.

I met a real life superhero, author Ty Allan Jackson, 2019.

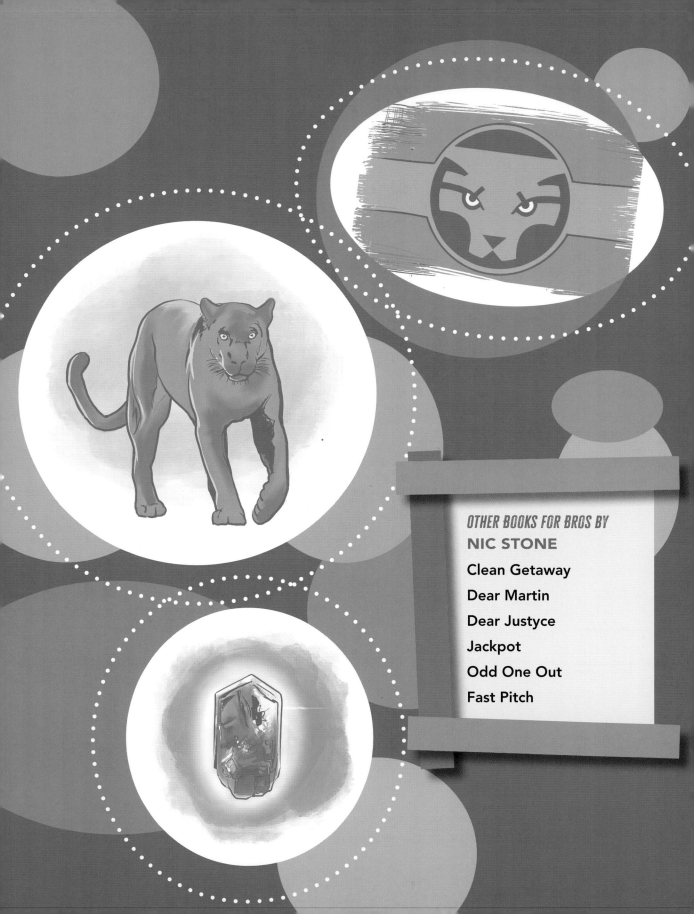

OTHER BOOKS FOR BROS BY
NIC STONE

Clean Getaway

Dear Martin

Dear Justyce

Jackpot

Odd One Out

Fast Pitch

SHURI
A Black Panther Novel

Written by **NIC STONE**

I have always been into comic books and graphic novels, but I didn't know about a black superhero until all the buzz started around the movie *Black Panther: Wakanda Forever.* It was a huge deal to the to Black community because now we had our own superhero and someone we can look up to who looked liked us. But maybe the best part about the movie is that it introduced us to another hero, Shuri.

If you have watched or read any of the Black Panther stories, you will be familiar with T'Challa's little sister, Shuri, who is a martial artist and genius. This novel, the first in a series, is about her growing up as a princess in Wakanda, a fictional country in Africa ruled by the T'Challa, the Black Panther. As a princess, Shuri breaks away from many of traditional roles women held in society. Shuri takes a liking to science, math, and engineering. And she becomes a fighter and sets out on a quest to save her homeland of Wakanda.

This book was inspiring for me, and I would imagine it is the same for girls who are interested in STEM (science, technology, engineering, and mathematics), but I recommend it to anyone.

Shuri was written by Nic Stone, one of my favorite authors, and whose book *Clean Getaway* was featured earlier.

While reading Shuri, I learned a lot more about her upbringing than what was told in the movies or comics. Her determination and brains allow for her to make her own legacy, and not be overshadowed by her older brother, the Black Panther. Girls often feel that they don't have a voice in a male-dominated society, and even more so, Black girls don't receive as many opportunities as others. That's why I feel that it is important for me to use my platform to advocate not only for Black boys but for girls too. Reading Shuri can inspire them to work for whatever it is they want in life and break down barriers in the process.

CHAPTER 5

FAMILY & COMMUNITY

Family and community are extremely important resources. You must do your best to preserve them no matter what, as they offer love, support, and protection. Personally, Books N Bros wouldn't have been successful without my community, one of the strongest and best. They've supported me in all of my endeavors, and I'm extremely grateful. Here I highlight some books that emphasize why, and how, family and community are important.

OUR FAMILY'S DOING YOGA

Written by **SONJORIA SYDNOR**
Illustrated by **DG**

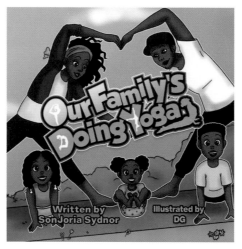

Our Family's Doing Yoga is a great book about a family of five. The children are very adventurous which leads to a lot of chaos, mess, and stress on their mother. Instead of taking a break away from the kids, the mother finds out about yoga, and the family decides to do yoga together as a way for everyone to find peace.

Our Family's Doing Yoga is an amazing book because not only is it a fun story about how a group activity changed a family and helped them bond, it's also a great way to learn about yoga and why it's good for you.

Throughout the story, the family practices yoga and stretch their bodies into different poses. A few of the poses the family tries are named after flowers and animals like the seated lotus, crane, and downward dog. Yoga doesn't look easy, but it sure does look fun.

And, at the end of the book, there is a guide that offers a description of a variety of yoga poses and visuals for how to do them on your own. In addition to the poses that we see the family do, other poses you can learn about include: butterfly, mountain, warrior, cobra, star, and many others. There are also recommendations for other activities like meditating and breathing that families can do together.

Our Family's Doing Yoga is only thirty-four pages with big and beautiful illustrations that stand out. It really is a quick read and it's told in rhyme, so it flows.

I find yoga to be truly fascinating. This book is a great introduction to yoga. And better yet, it's a useful tool for those times when you need to just relax and be calm.

ABC WHAT AN INFORMED VOTER YOU'LL BE!

Written by **MODERN KID PRESS**   Illustrated by **JACY CORRAL**

After reading the *March* series by John Lewis, who risked his life for African Americans to gain the right to vote, I had to read *ABC What an Informed Voter You Will Be* and recommend it for my Bros.

This is an important book because many of us kids aren't taught about how voting impacts our lives. If I'm being honest, civics and social studies are not the most fun subjects in school. But *ABC What an Informed Voter You Will Be* makes learning about these things easy to understand and you won't get bored.

The book provides an overview of American government, politics, and elections from A to Z. Each letter explains a topic. For example, A is for Affirmative Action, F is for First Amendment, P is for President, etc. It goes through the different ways voting affects big decisions like who becomes president, who civil rights are afforded to, and who gets to be a judge on the Supreme Court.

I think it's beneficial for kids to keep a copy of *ABC What an Informed Voter You Will Be* on their bookshelves because one day we will be old enough to vote. The more we know about what we are voting for, the more barriers we can overcome. Voting is an important responsibility of each American citizen, especially because everyone deserves to have a voice in shaping our society.

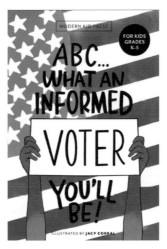

THE VOTING RIGHTS ACT OF 1965

Signed into law by President Lyndon B. Johnson, the Voting Rights Act of 1965 aimed to overcome barriers at state and local levels that prevented African Americans from exercising their right to vote as guaranteed by the U.S. Constitution. It is considered one of the most far-reaching pieces of civil rights legislation in U.S. history.

WE RISE, WE RESIST, WE RAISE OUR VOICES

Edited by **WADE HUDSON** and **CHERYL WILLIS HUDSON**

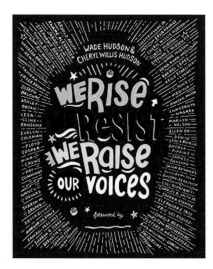

Personally, I love this book. It's one of those reads where you can sit down and read one story before bedtime. *We Rise, We Resist, We Raise Our Voices* is a collection of stories, poems, essays, letters, and a song by some of the most talented children's authors and activists including Kwame Alexander, Ellen Oh, and Rita Williams-Garcia, Jason Reynolds, Jacqueline Woodson, Carole Boston Weatherford, and more. Each story is paired with beautiful illustrations which adds another level of depth to the reading experience.

The book speaks to kids from marginalized communities, addressing a range of issues that they confront on an everyday basis, from stereotyping, racial profiling, and religious discrimination to community strength, empowerment, and resilience. What's great about this collection is that it allows you to see how some experiences are the same across race and religion.

Wade Hudson and Cheryl Wilson, who assembled the book's authors and illustrators, are the founders of Just Us Books. They founded Just Us over thirty years ago to publish books

FUN FACTS

Wade Hudson and Cheryl Willis Hudson are the publishers of Just Us Books, founded after they began searching for books that reflected the diversity of Black history, heritage and experiences for their own kids. They saw a need for books that Black children could relate to, and eventually started their own award-winning multicultural publishing company. They have partnered with many other publishers over the thirty years that they have been in business, with their belief that good books make a difference.

that reflect the lives of Black children. Books N Bros salutes Just Us Books for all they do.

Having a book that has short stories with characters who represent your identity is critical for Black kids to feel like they have a place in this world. Having a book like *We Rise, We Resist, We Raise Our Voices* is helpful for parents to give their children positive messages.

OTHER BOOKS FOR BROS BY
WADE HUDSON AND CHERYL WILLIS HUDSON

Great Black Heroes
Five Bold Freedom Fighters

Great Black Heroes
Five Notable Inventors

Great Black Heroes
Five Brave Explorers

The Talk
Conversations About Race, Love & Truth

Book of Black Heroes
Scientists, Healers & Inventors

Powerful Words
More Than 200 Years of Extraordinary Writing by African Americans

MARLEY DIAS GETS IT DONE

And So Can You!

Written by **MARLEY DIAS**

When I first found my voice in advocating for African American literacy, I soon learned about Marley Dias. The world was introduced to Marley after her appearance on the *Ellen Degeneres Show*. She had gotten noticed for starting the #1000BlackGirlBooks campaign when she was in the sixth grade. Marley couldn't connect with the books she was reading. So she decided to find one thousand books with characters that she could relate to. Sound familiar?

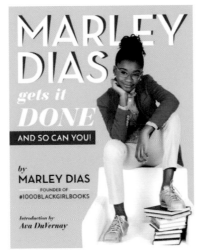

She's only one year older than me and we share many of the same passions. We are interested in social justice, advocacy, equity, literacy, and inclusion. I also find it cool how supportive her parents are. I relate to seeing her mom, Mrs. Janice Johnson-Dias, work closely with her as my mom has supported me.

In this book about her life, we see Marley navigate successfully along her journey of volunteerism, activism, and literacy with grace. But what's cool to me is how she wrote this book to show other kids that making a positive impact in their own communities can happen too. She takes readers step by step as she provides tips, tools, examples, and resources to guarantee success for anyone who reads this book to make the world a better place.

Marly Dias Gets It Done is honestly a literacy masterclass that lights the fire under any aspiring change agent to make their dream come true. Thank you Marley Dias for all you and your family have done.

FUN FACT

Activist and author Marley Dias was only eleven years old when she started #1000BlackGirlBooks!

OTHER BOOKS FOR BROS BY
STEWART MITCHELL

Kayla the Vegan

LIBERATION SUMMER

Written by **STEWART MITCHELL**

If you're looking for a novel that addresses animal cruelty, and certain fast-food chains in America that are strategically placed in under-served neighborhoods to sell unhealthy food to families, this is the book for you. *Liberation Summer* is written from the perspective of Jayden Young, a New Orleans teen who has graduated high school and will soon enter college. He decides to get a summer job at a popular fast-food restaurant, New Orleans Roasters, to help pay for his college tuition and books.

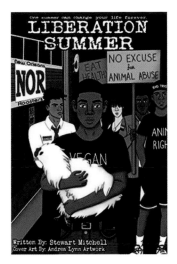

Jayden is an extremely likable and responsible character who gets along with everyone. He really loves sneakers, whether it's his Nike Air Force Ones or Jordans. And I can totally relate.

After Jayden gets the job at the restaurant, he becomes curious about where all the chicken comes from and why they get so much of it. So he decides to do some research into the meat industry. What he discovers about the treatment of animals changes his perspective of animal agriculture forever.

Liberation Summer opens our eyes to the unfortunate reality of animal cruelty and the existence of food deserts in low-income communities. Have you noticed if you live in or have traveled through an area that seems poorly cared for or abandoned, that there are rarely any grocery stores around? You may see a lot of corner stores and payday loan suppliers but there's hardly anywhere to get fresh vegetables and fruit. This is called a food desert. Many of us may live in or near one and may not realize it because we have transportation to get fresh food. Unfortunately, everyone doesn't have that luxury. And I appreciate Stewart Mitchell for bringing awareness to the issue.

After learning about how some of my favorite restaurants were contributing to this awful system, I became more mindful of what I was putting in my body and how livestock are treated.

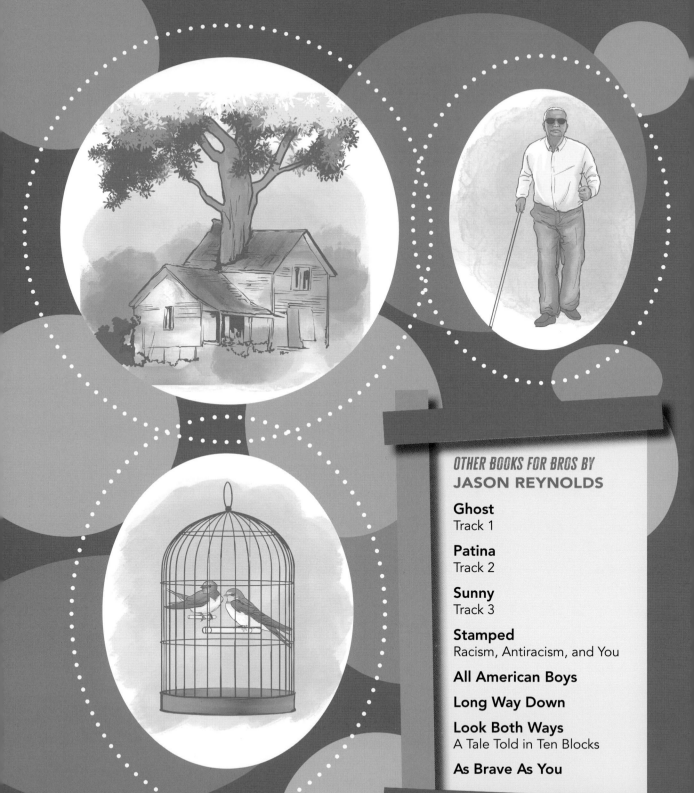

AS BRAVE AS YOU

Written by **JASON REYNOLDS**

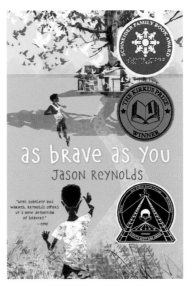

Because you can never have enough books by Jason Reynolds, here is one more.

As Brave As You is about two African American brothers, Genie and his older brother Ernie, whose parents are working on their relationship issues. To spend some time alone, they send the two brothers from Brooklyn, New York to Virginia to spend the summer with their grandparents. It's in Virginia that their adventure begins. And as boys will do, they get into a little trouble.

The story shows Genie and Ernie having to adjust to life in the country. They have to wake up early to do chores and work in the family's garden. The boys also have to get used to being around their grandfather Brooke who is blind. Brooke doesn't like going outside which is strange to Genie and Ernie.

The book though has some intense moments especially when Brooke, the blind grandfather, Genie, and Ernie have an incident involving a gun. What could go wrong, right? Assumptions are made about boyhood and manhood that force you to think about what real bravery means.

In addition to bravery, the book brings up difficult conversations around divorce, war-related PTSD (post-traumatic stress disorder), suicide, physical disabilities, and more. In fact, after reading the book, the Bros and I had in-depth conversations about issues we couldn't talk about at home.

This book contains some explicit language so if you're not ready for that, I'd say wait until you are mature enough to read it.

As Brave As You is one book that was perfect for the Bros because it's really all about family and relationships and how we grow with one another. You can't go wrong with this one.

CHAPTER 6

MONEY & CAREERS

Young entrepreneurs are necessary for the future—circulating money within our communities, educating youth about business, creating opportunities, and ultimately finding solutions to big problems as they get older. I believe despite your career choice, learning about money is essential. How to save, invest, and spend your money should be taught. Books are one way to do that, as you can see in this chapter.

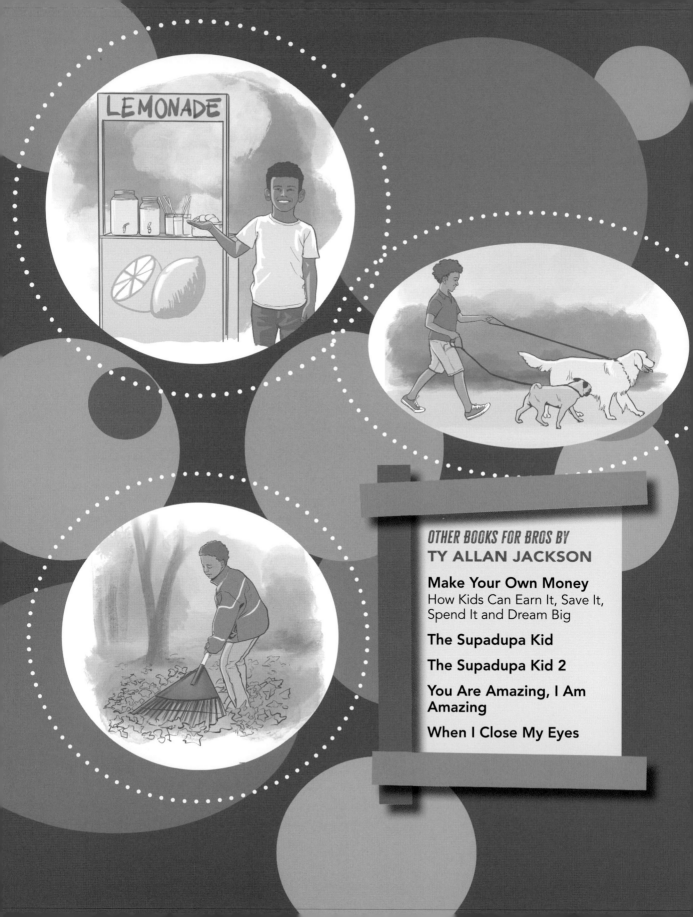

LEMONADE

OTHER BOOKS FOR BROS BY
TY ALLAN JACKSON

Make Your Own Money
How Kids Can Earn It, Save It,
Spend It and Dream Big

The Supadupa Kid

The Supadupa Kid 2

**You Are Amazing, I Am
Amazing**

When I Close My Eyes

DANNY DOLLAR MILLIONAIRE EXTRAORDINAIRE
The Lemonade Escapade

Written by **TY ALLAN JACKSON**

Danny Dollar Millionaire Extraordinaire is a fun book to read to learn about money. The main character, Danny, has big plans to become a millionaire, so he decides to do what many of us kids do when want to make money. He creates a lemonade stand. In order to do so, Danny reaches out to his mom to learn about different aspects of money and running a business.

I actually met the author Ty Allan Jackson. He shared with me that it was important for young readers, especially kids of color, to both learn about money and see themselves in the books they read. In fact, his book means a lot to me because it was the first book I read from EyeSeeMe African American Children's Bookstore in University City, Missouri, and it was the first book in the Books N Bros book club. I picked it up because

the boy on the cover looked like me.

The story takes you through Danny's daily life with his family, learning about finances, and how to save and invest his money from his lemonade stand. Some of the lessons Danny learns include: using a bank, setting up a savings account, interest charges, credit score, and much more. Maybe the best thing about the book is that it makes the reader think about how to spend money. Do you really want to buy $200-shoes or invest in a business?

Danny Dollar Millionaire Extraordinaire is a fun book to read and it makes learning about financial literacy a breeze with terms that are easy to understand.

Will Danny Dollar actually achieve his goal of becoming a millionaire? I guess you'll have to read the book to find out.

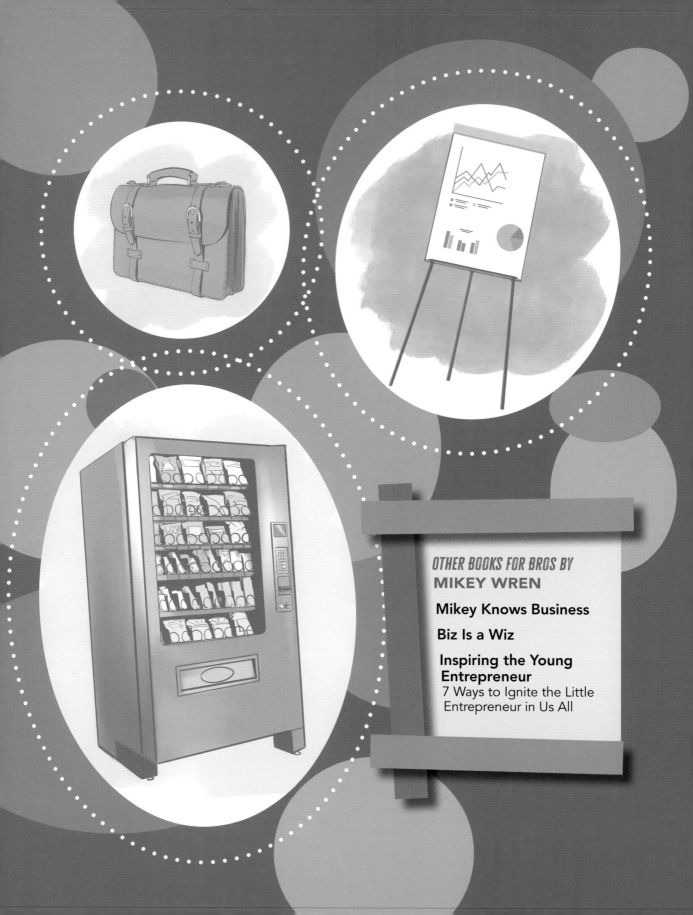

OTHER BOOKS FOR BROS BY
MIKEY WREN

Mikey Knows Business

Biz Is a Wiz

Inspiring the Young Entrepreneur
7 Ways to Ignite the Little Entrepreneur in Us All

MIKEY LEARNS ABOUT BUSINESS

Written by **MIKEY WREN**

Illustrated by **DONALD L. HILL, MBA**

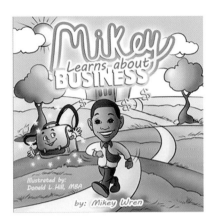

Mikey Learns about Business is a must-read book that was actually written by a friend of mine. He was one of the first Bros to attend a Books N Bros book club meeting. I soon learned that Mikey was an entrepreneur, and he was only seven or eight years old at the time. Incredible! Mikey wanted to own a vending machine as a source of income. He told his mom about his plan and together they made it happen. Inspired by Books N Bros, he then decided to write a book for kids. That book became *Mikey Learns about Business.*

At one of our Books N Bros meetups, this book opened discussions among the book club members about boys wanting to start their own businesses. It even inspired me to write my first book, *Cool Bros Read.*

In the book, nine-year-old Mikey, impressed by the amount of money spent on vending machine snacks, wants to own one for himself. But buying and running a vending machine business isn't as easy as it looks. When Mikey meets a magical briefcase named Biz, his dream of owning a business becomes even closer to becoming a reality.

Mikey Learns about Business teaches kids the basics of starting a business–how to write a business plan, raise money, market, network, and much more in a simple, easy-to-understand way.

I'm really grateful to Mikey for being one of the first Bros to support the book club and for sharing with us a beautiful story about realizing your dreams.

FUN FACT

Author and activist Mikey Wren is an inspirational young entrepreneur from St. Louis, Missouri, who is one of the youngest vending machine owners in the country. At the age of nine, he started his business, Mikey's Munchies, which now has twelve machines. He's on a mission to teach financial education and inspire entrepreneurship in kids like him!

THE TOOTHPASTE MILLIONAIRE

Written by **JEAN MERRILL**

The first thing to know about *The Toothpaste Millionaire* is that it was written in 1972. That's fifty years ago! Still, the book is relevant today and a great way to learn about business.

In the book, sixth-grader Rufus Mayflower thinks that toothpaste is too expensive and like most people, he just wants to save money wherever he can. He makes a bet with a friend that he can make more toothpaste than what is found in the store and sell it for a cheaper price. To his surprise, Rufus' toothpaste is a hit and now he has to figure out how to make enough to fulfill orders. Supply

and demand.

While Rufus isn't in it for the money, he succeeds, and that's where I relate to this as a young entrepreneur. Yes I aim to be successful and you have to make money in business, but I never want to get lost in money-driven things.

As a young entrepreneur, *The Toothpaste Millionaire* was such an inspiration for me, and it's also a trailblazer for many other wonderful children's books about financial literacy like *Danny Dollar Millionaire* and *Mikey Learns about Business*.

FUN FACT

Author Jean Merrill wrote more than thirty books in her lifetime! Her inspiration? She says, "the great impact certain books had on me as a child, and perhaps a wish to recreate the quality of that experience."

CONCLUSION
A Note from Mom

Hey there! Winnie here, a.k.a. Sidney's mom, a.k.a. momager and co-pilot of this literary life journey. I thought it was important for me to dive in here, as our journey has been so poetic as a mother-son duo.

January 31, 2006, a noteworthy date, is when I gave birth to Sidney Keys III. I'd just turned 17 two weeks prior and had no idea that being his mother would change my outlook on life the way it has—especially regarding literacy. I remember receiving mail about the Mickey Mouse Club books, and Dr. Seuss as the silent invitation to every baby into the literacy world. It wasn't until Sidney was ten years old, and home from his first solo flight after visiting my mother in California for three weeks, that I had a major surprise for him. I took him to an African American children's bookstore in St. Louis because I knew how much he loved reading; but most importantly I recognized how much he hadn't seen himself in books as a brilliant young Black boy.

Now that he's in high school, I'm in awe of the opportunities that advocating for African American literacy have allowed us as servants in this space. Whether it be personal or professional decisions, books have been our footstools to success in this journey.

Never in a million years did we think literacy would have impacted our lives as it has. Advocating for literature, especially African American literature, has been a journey we'll continue as long as time allows. Reaching hundreds of boys in our Books N Bros membership and millions of people thanks to supporters and media outlets, we've helped many learn to love reading again. Even as we collectively worked on this project, we can confidently say that writing this book has even lit a fire beneath us to continue advocating. Our personal mission is to serve as we're called to, and also not accept Sidney as an anomaly but an example to any Black boy, that he can be whoever he wants to be and travel anywhere while doing so.

Additionally, to the parents supporting their kids in entrepreneurship, it is hard. Managing your child every day won't be all glitter and

unicorns. But ultimately, parent, is your number one role. Working with Sidney has allowed him to see me as human. We've gotten lost in books together. We've been blessed to travel to advocate for African American literacy together. But there were days where

My mother speaking at EyeSeeMe bookstore in St. Louis. For our workshops, she would host conversations with educators, parents, and students to share the journey of Books N Bros and inspire attendees to go after their dreams!

I had to remove the momager hat. Sidney is my child first, and he always shows up at his best when he's seen, safe, and protected. That, my friends, is success in a parent-child working relationship and I wouldn't trade our experience for the world.

RESOURCES

BOOK CLUBS TO WATCH

For Youth
- Project Lit Community
- Nerdy Girlz Book Club
- Friends of Cabrini Virtual

Book Club For Adults
- Black Men Read
- DiversaTea Reads
- For Colored Girls Book Club, Brown Folks Book Circle, and Mocha Girls Rea

LITERACY SUBSCRIPTION BOXES THAT FOCUS ON BLACK STORIES

- Just Like Me Box
- Eye See Me Subscription box
- Because of Them We Can box
- A Kids Book box by A Kids Co.

LITERARY RESOURCES

- **Young Black and Lit**—Providing books featuring Black characters to local youth for free

- **Turn The Page STL**—Spearheading the initiative dedicated to increasing the number of children that are reading at or above grade level by the end of third grade.

- **The Brown Bookshelf**—The Brown Bookshelf is an online resource that promotes awareness of Black children's book creators (including YA).

- **Turn the Page KC**—Turn the Page KC is to mobilize our entire community to ensure children gain the literacy skills they need to create a lifetime of opportunity, regardless of what school they attend or what zip code they are from.

- **Auburn Avenue Research Library**—Located in Atlanta, GA, this is the first library in the Southeast to offer specialized reference dedicated to the research of African American culture and African descent.

ACKNOWLEDGMENTS

We would like to thank all the supporters and contributors who have helped us get to where we are today. In no particular order, we would like to take this opportunity to specifically acknowledge some of you.

All of the founding Books N Bros members: You all believed in us from seven members to serving almost 700 members. You saw the vision clearer than us at times. Thank you for pushing us to stick to it!

Deborah "Grandmommy" Sistrunk-Nelson: The first woman to push both my mom and I to read. Thank you for being a beautiful example and contributing so much knowledge to us personally and professionally.

Ishmael Sistrunk: Uncle Ishmael, thank you for always showing up. Sometimes that's all that us Bros needed and you have been committed since day one.

Marwin: Let's talk about unwavering faith. Thank you for helping us manage everything since you've entered our lives. You have been so selfless and loving. We couldn't be here happy, healthy, and whole without you.

Jerika: From day one you had no problem pulling up your bootstraps to support our dreams and the needs of our Bros. We always know, if Jerika is there, it's getting done. Thank you now and forever.

Richelle: Our therapist and how we've managed such a mindset-changing journey. Thanks for reminding us individually to keep ourselves at the front of our own equation.

Ashlee Nicole: You're one of the few people to see the lows in addition to the highs. Thank you for offering your expertise and skills to help us sustain our efforts.

Steve and Marjorie Harvey: When you said we were going to blow up, you never lied. Thank you both for believing in us.

Eemerg Roadside Assistance: Your love and investment in us will always be appreciated.

EyeSeeMe African American Children's Bookstore: You're forever in our hearts and hold a permanent place in our literacy family. Thank you for your willingness, support and kindness.

Caldwell and Sistrunk family: Thank you for your support and love!

Marks family: Thank you for seeing us with your hearts and supporting us as the allies we never knew we needed. Love you forever.

Alexander family: You all have offered a space of laughter, labor and love. We are forever grateful.

Ferguson Youth Initiative: Your mission is to keep youth at the center. For allowing us to use your space to reach families in Ferguson and neighboring areas, we thank you.

Keys family: Thank you for supporting our endeavors, near and far. A special shoutout to my Dad and Granddad for always rooting for us.

Jim Brown: You're truly an angel on earth. Thank you for everything.

Doss: As a friend, mentor, and big bro, thank you for showing up and being the best you.

Amira: Your support and commitment to Books N Bros is unmatched. Thank you forever.

Onwubiko family: Even when it didn't make sense, you stood beside us. That calls for a huge hug. Thank you.

Kathy and Corion: You were the first family to show us that Books N Bros is more than a book club, we're a community, a family. We love you both. Thank you.

Rob Liano: You met us at a pivotal moment. It was hard. You gave us hope to push through. You are forever cherished.

Melanie: Darren would be proud of us all.

Mrs. Cramer: The best fifth-grade teacher ever, thank you for seeing in us what we needed to see in ourselves.

Mr. G: Thank you for being a safe space for me and my mom as a mother-son duo trying to balance the life that's been assigned to us.

Biggs family: You never ask for acknowledgment but you deserve as many thanks as life allows. You're family. We love you. We thank you.

Danyelle: Thank you for pushing us, giving access to all platforms that made sense and for fulfilling any vision you've had in supporting us. Greatest of all time.

Gerard: From sports, to education, to Books N Bros, you always show up. Thank you.

Tanya, Dara, and Eva: Whenever we can't handle the low lows or the high highs, you're available at either end. You all are truly the fairy God muva.

Brianca: You're always one call away. And also the hype woman we will love forever.

Valeria: Your compassion for us and investment is always appreciated. We love you!

OTHER BOOKS FROM OUR TOMORROW
A BOOK SERIES WRITTEN BY YOUNG COMMUNITY LEADERS AND ACTIVISTS, DEDICATED TO INSPIRING, UPLIFTING, AND EMPOWERING THE NEXT GENERATION OF LEADERS

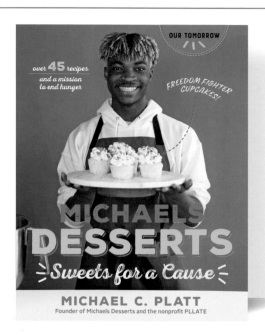

MICHAELS DESSERTS
Sweets for a Cause (Michael Platt)

A fun cookbook for all ages by teen baker, social entrepreneur, and food justice advocate Michael C. Platt, inspired by his mission to end food insecurity one dessert at a time. Recipes include No Kid Hungry French Toast Breakfast Cupcakes, Nelson Mandela Malva Pudding Cupcakes, and Booker T. Washington Vegan Chocolate Cupcakes.

ISBN 9781684620470

KINDNESS IS MY HOBBY
How to Change the World Right Where You Are (Ruby Kate Chitsey)

Ruby Kate Chitsey, the teenage founder and CEO of Three Wishes for Ruby's Residents, shares how she spreads kindness every day and how you can do it too, with activities inspired by her own initiatives that have gained her national attention. Projects include Senior Pen Pal Project, Mobile Book Cart, and Postcards of Kindness.

ISBN 9781684620609